"Transforming ... ...ch desperately needs. Until we recover a healthy doctrine of the Church, joined with a practical concern for the life of community in the Church, we will never see significant biblical reformation. Mark Lauterbach's love for the Church is passionate and realistic. He has the courage to address her need for correction and the tough love to do it superbly. This is the best contemporary book on Church discipline I have read."

John H. Armstrong, President,
Reformation & Revival Ministries
Carol Stream, IL

"Mark Lauterbach has written a biblically sensitive and pastorally wise book on a subject many people would just as soon forget about: accountability among Christians. True church discipline is not about reinforcing legalisms but rather nurturing believers within a covenanted community of faith. Loving discipline leads to transformation and this, I believe, is a prerequisite for the kind of revival we are praying for and so desperately need."

Timothy George, Dean,
Beeson Divinity School,
Samford University, Birmingham, AL

"I have never read a book like this or even one close to this. Mark Lauterbach writes with a rare combination of biblical insight and seasoned compassion born of many years "in the trenches" of local church leadership. What he says about church discipline is not theoretical (as much books on the subject tend to be) but pastoral in the deepest and best sense of the word. He properly sets church discipline in the larger context of God's grace and the messy reality of ongoing human sinfulness. This is not so much a "how-to" manual (though there is plenty of good advice here) as it is a practical guide through the maze of imperfect people who make foolish choices, sometimes over and over again, and how the church should deal with them. I found myself nodding in agreement over and again. If you think church discipline is outdated or irrelevant in the 21st century, Mark Lauterbach will convince you otherwise. Pastor, read this book! Then buy copies for every pastor on your staff and for every person on your governing board."

**Dr. Ray Pritchard, Senior Pastor
Calvary Memorial Church, Oak Park, IL**

'Transforming Communities aredesperately needed today and I applaud this helpful contribution to their recovery.'

**Luder G. Whitlock, Jr., President
Excelsis**

THE
TRANSFORMING COMMUNITY
THE PRACTISE OF THE GOSPEL IN CHURCH DISCIPLINE
MARK LAUTERBACH

Reformation & Revival Ministries

CHRISTIAN FOCUS

Dr. Mark Lauterbach is a graduate of Princeton University, Western Seminary, and Trinity Evangelical Divinity School. He has been married for almost 25 years and has three children. To keep sane, he plays golf. Since 1981 he has served in pastoral ministry in established churches and has volunteered in various missions agencies. He is currently training for church planting work. He has written articles for Leadership and Reformation and Revival Jounrals. His preaching is aired on the Sunday Worship Hour with Family Radio.

Dedication

To the congregation of El Camino Baptist.
Thanks for joining the Lord in becoming a
transforming community.

© Mark Lauterbach

ISBN 1 85792 875 X

Published in 2003
by
Christian Focus Publications Ltd,
Geanies House, Fearn,
Ross-shire, IV20 1TW,
Great Britain
and
Reformation & Revival Ministries Inc,.
P.O. Box 88216
Carol Stream, Illinois 60188 USA

www.christianfocus.com

Cover design by Alister MacInnes

Printed and bound by
Cox & Wyman, Reading, Berkshire

All rights reserved. No part of this publication may be reproduced, stored in a retrieval system, or transmitted, in any form, by any means, electronic, mechanical, photocopying, recording or otherwise without the prior permission of the publisher or a license permitting restricted copying. In the U.K. such licenses are issued by the Copyright Licensing Agency, 90 Tottenham Court Road, London W1P 9HE.

Contents

Preface

A Church for Our Times

I shall start, then, with the church, into whose bosom God is pleased to gather his sons, not only that they may be nourished by her help and ministry as long as they are infants and children but also that they may be guided by her motherly care until they mature and at least reach the goal of faith. . . . so that, for those to whom he is Father the church may also be Mother.

John Calvin

*****

When we built our first house in the Arizona desert, the contractor labored on the foundation. I used to go out for visits and became impatient with the process. It seemed as though weeks passed with not much visible result. Some wood framing established the lines of the concrete pour. Plumbing was roughed in and electrical supply routed through a pipe. Then long pieces of steel were laid out like a grid through this space. It took days for the rebar to be put in place. One day I found the result – this concrete slab stretched out, with various pieces of pipe protruding from its flat terrain. That was it.

What I did not know was that all this work was essential to the home we would inhabit. Contractors had learned some lessons. They had always taken care with foundations, but this was different. Invisible layers of silt lace their way through desert soils. During rainy seasons, these layers shift and slide. Tucson's valley floor moved endlessly. When layers migrated, the concrete resting on them gave way. People found their homes divided. One man told us of the crevasse which formed in his living room, the tearing up of carpet, and the drilling for new concrete piers to support his divided home. Lawsuits later, builders learned to reinforce the slab, weaving thick metal rebar throughout the poured cement.

I have come to believe that people are like concrete, fairly secure in times of stability, but fragile in times of change. They need reinforcement. We live in such times. In previous centuries the culture provided reinforcement for breakable human lives. Everyone agreed: marriage was inviolable, families stayed together, and honor was shown to the elderly. A man's word was his bond. Sexuality was covered and private. Certain public behavior was shameful. A clear and ordered world of truth and certainties wove itself through the fabric of our souls, providing strength for the shifting soils of their day. Such conditions produced persons with some measure of social integrity and fixed principles.

In the West such convictions are a faint memory. One American author has even written of the death of character. James Davison Hunter believes that the culture we inhabit cannot produce great character.

Dr. Hunter has argued that the desire to cultivate integrity is little more than a pipe dream for the twenty-first century citizen of the western world. The environmental conditions, which breed people of character, are gone. Rejection of all truth claims, the assertion of personal self-determination, the iconoclasm of the new generation, the dissolution of marriage and family: these coalesce in a foul soil, good for nothing but the worst of weeds. This is where we live!

I have a growing sense that Hunter is right. The reinforcements of culture, which kept us from being brittle, are gone. We are fragile people. People's choices brutalize their own souls. Their exercised freedom leaves pain in its wake. The unbelieving are not naïve about evil. They have tasted its power and rule.

At the time of my ordination, my friend and mentor in ministry pulled me aside. "Mark," he predicted, "in your ministry years, you will see more sin in a year among Christians than I have seen in thirty. Be prepared for the battle." My friend was not an historian, but he understood the times. That was over twenty years ago. He was not a prophet but he was correct.

Here are some of the sins I have faced in twenty plus years of pastoral ministry: adultery in leadership, incest, abuse of wives and children, rape, embezzlement, drug and alcohol abuse, sex change surgeries, fornication, and homosexuality. Rather than being infrequent occurrences, these are regular happenings. I have seen these evils in all ages and stages of life, at all levels of maturity in believers. I have watched elders resign over trivial differences, staff members depart in dishonorable ways, charter members lead a movement against a new pastor, and lawsuits filed by missionaries against a mission. These are not the sins of the pagan world but of God's people. I have said at times that I would rather face persecution rather than a deceptive leader or divisive member. Friendly fire is far more painful.

The good news is that these have provided a context for learning, a laboratory for the application of Scripture to the order of church life and the mending of sin-torn lives. I am glad to report that God's Spirit still does his work in human lives, no matter how intense the sin and how damaging. I am sorry to report that when the church ceases to be the church and functions as a corporation or a club, few lives are touched by the Spirit of God.

As a pastor I ask: what does it mean to be the people of Jesus Christ in such a world? How effective are we in penetrating the lives of those around us with the Good News of Jesus crucified and raised? What does it mean to be the bride of Jesus in this time?

Preface

I believe Christianity is robust enough to face these days with confidence and effectiveness. I believe that the church is called to be a unique people in all cultures and at all times. We are the blood-bought new human race, in Christ, under the Gospel, waiting the day of consummation. We live in the last chapter of the old order.

I write to pastors who have given up hope and jettisoned an ordered pursuit of holiness from their churches. Lay leaders should read as well, for pastors cannot go it alone in seeking to bring order to a local church. In addition, members should read and support their leaders by obedience.

Here is the problem. We need a model that suits our times. Moreover, I think that model is buried in the Scriptures. It has died for want of attention.

Where I live in America two options currently present themselves. First, there are churches addicted to a style of ministry that was designed for a different society than our own. It is controlled by concerns about image, putting on a good face, seeking to recover the golden era of post World War America, when men were men and women knew their place. Back then, it is believed, people were moral and honest. These churches live in an illusion. They are not places where people may confess their sin safely. They believe that perfect lives are the best commendation for the Gospel. They are filled with believers who work out their salvation with desperation. Everyone else seems to be so together, and they are not. These churches are fewer in number than a decade ago, and this is good news.

Second, there is a growing population of churches seeking institutional fixes by creating more attractive billboards. These churches follow a corporation model of focused vision and purpose, defined program and activity. There is usually a higher priority to reality in these local assemblies, and people are freer to confess their failings. Support groups for all manner of addictions are available and attendance is encouraged.

This is a step in the right direction. However, often these churches jettison the type of tough love discipline and admonition that is crucial to true holiness. Confession and support are great for our needs. But is there accountability? If you are a member of such a church, let me ask you this: when was the last time you knew of someone being rebuked for their sins? Alternatively, when was someone removed from the membership because of persistent unrepentant transgressions?

Both models are extremely institutional and call upon pastors to be CEO's. Both channel ministry through the conduit of program, and secondarily through relationships. I think there is a better option and have seen its effectiveness.

So, what's the church to be? Are we to be perfect communities of smiling saints who look past each other on the Lord's Day? Should we be shocked when believers stumble into sin? On the other hand, should we design new programs where we can talk to people's problems without getting involved, leaving them to figure it out on their own after the lecture hall empties? Should we hand over all the real messiness to the professionals and keep the church out of the muck?

I am not an idealist. I have been in the trenches for two decades. I am quite aware that there are no perfect churches. Every church has problems. However, I am also aware that people use that as an excuse for the status quo. Every church has problems. Not all problems are equally serious. It is like marriage. Some are on the edge of divorce, and others work out their problems daily or weekly.

My concern is not that we create perfect churches but that we have in place the right metrics for assessing where there are problems and the right principles for addressing them. I believe the model of Scripture is adequate. It speaks realistically and redemptively to the lives of saints. It addresses the "how to" of forming a growing and honest community of believers.

I believe that a local church, pursuing biblical fellowship and ordering its life under Scripture, is powerful in the hands of the Spirit to change lives. I have seen this at work. The church has all the rebar of Gospel truth needed to reinforce the brittle concrete of people's lives.

The church should be a place that engages with people's lives. Everything about a local church should be "real." We should have a sign over our door that reads: "Bring your problems with you." We must be places that get our hands dirty. Pastors and elders must emerge from their studies and be involved with people personally. We need more shepherds and fewer ranchers.

I think Jesus is our model for ministry. Throughout his ministry they brought to him the lepers, the diseased, the demonized, the paralyzed, the blind and he had compassion on them and healed them. He taught publicly and rebuked privately. He was a physician of the soul.

This is a portrait of all of us. Thanks to Adam's sin, we are all lepers. I know no healthy persons, only lepers. Spurgeon noted that we are all a little off balance. How true. Jesus miracles were the one normal thing in a world of the abnormal.

This is what the church, his body, is to do in every local congregation. The ministry of the church is the application of the Gospel in truth, compassion, and engagement. Compassion is the only godly response to a world of lepers, ruined by sin. Engagement means we cease to minister at a safe distance, instead we touch people's lives. We call them to holiness and we do so face to face.

I believe all the grace of Jesus Christ can be mediated through a functioning body of believers. Members can be encouraged to move past programs and wade into the mess of life with each other. This is not to be problem-centered, self-obsessed ministry. It is Christ-centered, compassionate, holy, and engaged with life. "Let's encourage each other on the journey of holiness." It is not simplistic sloganeering (just stop being depressed, pray about it and move on), but the simplicity of Christ shoulder-deep in human complexity. Through the sweat and toil of that kind of community Jesus will work in people's lives.

Preface

Some say, "Just preach the Word and all will be well." Richard Baxter long ago proved that to be a flawed method. It is not enough to preach. Baxter found that few remembered his preaching. However, when he came close and worked with families and individuals, permanent change took place. There must be engagement by pastors who cease to be CEO's, but this too is not enough.

Wesley and Whitfield both preached, but one left a movement that has endured for two hundred years. Wesley brought converts together in cells where tough and humbling questions were asked, faults were discussed, and specific sins were confessed. This is engagement by members with each other.

I believe in the local church. I believe in it as a redemptive, healing community. As a pastor I have seen deep bondage broken by a church being the church.

I have watched elderly people surround an alcoholic friend with tough love and prayer. He had returned to his drunkenness in his retirement, while his wife was suffering deeply. They stepped into his life and God used them. The church prayed. Today he is free.

I watched a group of ladies become the intercessors for a woman diagnosed with Multiple Personality Disorders. Today she is a functioning believer in a local church. I have seen a man confess to felonies before a church, shameful sexual indecency. Today he is walking with Jesus.

I have also witnessed the long term effects of church life where people hide their sin, sweep conflicts under the rug, ask dissenters to leave, and refuse to make confession and restitution where there is wrong. They live to protect their reputation and each others egos. Their motto: "It's in the past, it's behind us."

The result of such self-protective disobedience is a church infested with mistrust, indirect communication, gossip, and power plays. No one dared step forward for help and no one would do the tough work of accountability. Pastors were program managers. Few lives were changed. It reminded me of country clubs where I played golf as a child and teenager.

Jesus clarified the nature of the local assembly in his earliest words about the church, in Matthew 18. This is the passage about church discipline. I think of it as the passage that tells how to maintain the health of the body of Christ by treating the diseases of sin that arise, sometimes even to the point of removing a cancer. However, in so many cases there will be life-changing repentance when we face sin and apply the resources of Christ and His body.

We will begin with the big picture. For three chapters we will consider a satellite shot of the church. What is she? What is the mission of the church? What attitudes should govern us? Knowing who we are in Christ determines why we should pursue these practices.

We will then move piece by piece through the passage on church discipline in Matthew, taking it apart, setting it in its broader context, and working out application. The danger is to find in it a simplistic formula. It is not.

Each of the chapters of this book is like a self-contained sermon. This means that it has an interest in focusing on a particular point but also gives the whole picture to keep faithful to the plan of God and keep that before the reader. Bear with the repetition that may be necessary.

However, there is a great deal of difference between a set of directions and skillful implementation of them. My children obtained a swing set many years ago. I had to assemble it. The directions were clear and quite simple compared to some. Still, it was three hours before I had assembled anything that looked like a swing.

I called for a friend, experienced and gifted in such things. Within a half hour of his arrival, it was ready for us. It was not the directions that made the difference; it was his experience he brought to bear on the parts.

It is the same with church discipline. My goal is to help others assemble the parts in ways that are more helpful. I wish to do this by using the realities of church life as I have known it or observed nearby.

I want to describe the method of Christ for dealing with troubled lives and show that it is anything but institutional. It is intensely hands on. It is not a program, but a personal involvement with each other. However, we need to know what that looks like. There is much talk today about the church being a community. I hope to show what it will look like in practice.

This could be seen as a book on Church Discipline. It is really a book about Spirit-empowered Community. Church discipline is not something we "do" to someone in sin. Church discipline is the constant activity of a church where holiness and love are pursued. We should always be watching over each other, encouraging each other daily against the possibility of a hardened heart, stimulating each other toward love and good works. We should always be facing sin head on in the Gospel. Such a pattern was the function of the apostolic church where people came from similarly messed up lives as we face today. God used them. We must be realistic about the mess and hopeful because of Christ.

I have great hope. The church is an emergency room for the sin-sick souls that live in the twenty-first century. Local bodies are the instruments of the Spirit for ministering the redemption of Jesus. The church should be a safe place where the believing can come and not have to put on their Sunday best. Those who admit sickness should find help.

They should come and find brothers and sisters who welcome them in the name of Jesus and point them to Jesus. The leaders should assure the members that the church is a place to face the troubles of their own souls and to be strengthened in godliness.

Preface

Such churches do not just happen. Building such local assemblies will take courage and work. Most of all, it will take a vision of the beauty of Christ's body and bride.

1

New Community

Accordingly, as the saving doctrine of Christ is the soul of the church, so does discipline serve as its sinews, through which the members of the body hold together, each in its own place. Therefore, all who desire to remove discipline or to hinder its restoration – whether they do this deliberately or out of ignorance – are surely contributing to the ultimate dissolution of the church.

John Calvin

*****

Let us start with part one of the big picture. Remember the story of the bricklayers in London centuries ago? There, in the heart of London, they labored, constructing a wall. Hour after hour and day after day they plumbed the wall, leveled the cement, and added one more layer of bricks. A passer by asked the men what they were doing. One man replied, "We are building a wall." The other demurred, "No, he said, we are assisting Sir Christopher Wren in building a Cathedral."

Perspective makes all the difference in the world. Have you ever tried to assemble a jigsaw puzzle without the picture on the box? Contractors work off blueprints. Blueprints are the big picture. How do you see the blueprint for the church? What picture are you working from when you assemble the church? I have usually found that pastors and members have different blueprints.

Some of the laity may picture the church as a place to go for inspiration and friendship. If they have a family, they look for programs for their kids. They want the right music, the right kind of pastor, and the right kind of people to meet. Members can be loyal. They hang in there as long as certain lines are not crossed. If they are unhappy they may protest by holding back their giving. They may criticize and undermine the leadership. Everyone has a different line which cannot be crossed. I know one man who left a church because they quit giving free donuts to the volunteers on Saturday morning. He thought that was petty. Some members figure they can outlast pastors, even if they are unhappy.

Pastors picture church as a place for ministry. They want to serve people and help them grow in Christ. They design programs to do so. That is a great challenge. Some churches want a chaplain, not a pastor who leads them. The members own the church. They live with the tension between living up to people's expectations and the plan of God. They walk on the razor's edge of preserving tradition and exercising leadership. Ambition creeps in and fouls the waters. Pastoral ego is no minor matter. Most pastors aspire to be successful, to have a large church, and to be like the latest guru in church work. Pastors love their congregations. They take pleasure in being part of people's lives. They are especially delighted when lives change.

I think both of these lack vision. They are tiny and shriveled. They are both the perspective of the first bricklayer. The church is so much more. Christ is doing a wonderful work.

We are a new people. My understanding of the New Testament and the flow of biblical history is that the church is the consummation of God's purposes. In Creation, God established his kingdom. In sin, that kingdom was disrupted and humanity rebelled against their King. The story line of salvation in history is that God determined to create a new human race, a new people, who would be his kingdom and his people in everlasting ages. The Lord of heaven invaded this world, took on human flesh, and plundered the kingdom of darkness. He exposed the heart of the usurper, Satan. With every miracle he revealed his heart as generous and kind. By his death, he broke the legal hold of the devil's reign. In Adam, all of humanity came to death. In Christ, the new head of the human race, we are all recreated.

It is this to which the Gospel speaks. Jesus came, suffered, and died, not to save an individual here or there, but to make a people of his own. He was rescuing from the mass of the fallen world of humans a new human race, redeemed at the cost of his blood, and recreated by his Spirit. In his death, he brought an end to the old order. It is in its last chapter. In his resurrection he began that new kingdom. The church at this time lives in the overlap of the old age and the new age. We are rescued from this present evil age by his death. We are made a kingdom of priests. We are being built into a holy temple of the Lord. This is hard to see, but essential.

I have wondered for years how the argument of Paul in Romans seems to be sidelined in the middle of chapter five. This lengthy treatment of the contrast between Adam and Christ seems to be a tangent (5:12–21).

> If, because of one man's trespass, death reigned through that one man, much more will those who receive the abundance of grace and the free gift of righteousness reign in life through the one man Jesus Christ. Therefore, as one trespass led to condemnation for all men, so one act of righteousness leads to justification and life for all men. For as by the one man's disobedience the many were made sinners, so by the one man's obedience the many will be made righteous.
> (Rom. 5:17–19).

The passage speaks to the imputation of Adam's sin upon the entire human race. It addresses the purpose of God, that in Christ, all the effects of

Adam's sin will be reversed and overcome. Death reigns through Adam; the grace of God through Christ reigns in life.

Paul repeats this a number of times. The weighty section comes to a happy conclusion: "as sin reigned in death, grace also might reign through righteousness leading to eternal life through Jesus Christ our Lord."

Having preached this a number of times I dreaded this section, and did my best to make the sermon short and simple. The eyes of my people glazed over as I spoke. I focused on the latter part and assured them of forgiveness. I also completely missed the point.

Paul, I believe, is guarding against a small picture of salvation. He does not want us to think that all God is doing in Christ is rescuing individuals from sin and condemnation. He does not want us to think that heaven will be a world of unrelated individuals somehow being acquainted for the first time. His point is: Christ is the One who reverses the ruin of the old creation. He establishes a kingdom of righteousness by his blood. He turns death backward. We are part of the new creation. Grace shall reign through us in righteousness forever.

We may use another biblical picture to understand this. The story of Noah is a story of judgment of the old and a new beginning. Through a new "Adam and Eve" the command is given again to be fruitful, multiply, fill the earth, and subdue it. This was a new human race. In addition, it grew by procreation. There are two differences between this and the church. First, it failed. Noah was a son of Adam and his children inherited the corruption of sin and the reign of death. The power of Adam's sin was not broken. In Christ it is. Second, it grew by procreation. The new human race allows for no children and grandchildren. Each is born of God by the Spirit.

This is very hard for an American to grasp. Our understanding of being "us" before we are "me" is weak. Even our families are increasingly a collection of individuals coexisting under the same roof. Meals are not taken together. I have learned about this from brothers and sisters from other parts of the world.

Another picture of the corporate identity of the church is given by Peter.

> you yourselves like living stones are being built up as a spiritual house, to be a holy priesthood, to offer spiritual sacrifices acceptable to God through Jesus Christ. (1 Pet. 2:5).

The Apostle pictures the church as a Living Temple, being built of living stones, with Christ as the cornerstone. He goes on to speak of the church in "corporate" terms:

> But you are a chosen race, a royal priesthood, a holy nation, a people for his own possession, that you may proclaim the excellencies of him who called you out of darkness into his marvelous light (1 Pet. 2:9).

All of these are in the plural. Most commands in the New Testament are in the plural.

The church is a glorious, functioning body, of which Christ is the head. Let's consider Paul's letter to the Ephesians and its teaching. He ends chapter one with a prayer, within which is a request that they will know the measure of God's power for them. He describes that power as revealed in the resurrection and exaltation of Jesus:

> that he worked in Christ when he raised him
> from the dead and seated him at his right hand
> in the heavenly places, far above all rule and
> authority and power and dominion, and above
> every name that is named, not only in this age
> but also in the one to come.
> (Eph. 1:20–21, ESV).

I think it is significant that Paul speaks here of the age to come. This is the age of the Messianic kingdom, when old things are passed away and all things will be new. This is where the new humanity will dwell in their glory.

Paul then goes on to note the relationship of Christ to the church: "And he put all things under his feet and gave him as head over all things to the church, which is his body, the fullness of him who fills all in all." (Eph. 1:22–23). The exalted Lord of the universe is made head of the church. And what is the church? It is his body. It is his fullness.

I like the way Eugene Peterson has paraphrased Ephesians 1:22–3. "At the center of this, Christ rules the church. *The church, you see, is not peripheral to the world; the world is peripheral to the church"* (*The Message*[1], my emphasis).

The church is more important than the internet revolution, more significant than the politics of the Middle East, more valuable than the wealth of the great economic powers. These are on the sidelines of God's great work. The action is the church. Everything else is a spectator. No matter how small the local congregation, this is true.

I was taught for years that the church was a parenthesis in the purposes of God. The real action was between Israel and God. This passage tells me otherwise. How can a parenthesis be the fullness of Christ?

In the rest of Ephesians Paul fills us in on the significance of the church. Paul fills in the word with immense meaning. He starts with the purpose of Christ in his sacrifice, "that he might create in himself one new man in place of the two, so making peace" (Eph. 2:15) We are the "new man," the new creation humanity, made up of Jews and Gentiles. All distinctions of the older covenant are done away. There is not Jew or Gentile in Christ. The old creation is being done away.

> So then you are no longer strangers and aliens,
> but you are fellow citizens with the saints and
> members of the household of God, built on
> the foundation of the Apostles and prophets,
> Christ Jesus himself being the cornerstone, in

---

1. *The Message*, Eugene Peterson, NavPress, Colorado Springs, CO, 2002

> whom the whole structure, being joined
> together, grows into a holy temple in the Lord.
> In him you also are being built together into
> a dwelling place for God by the Spirit
> (Eph. 2:19–22).

We are the household of God. Christ is our cornerstone. We are the temple, the final dwelling of God, the most holy place. That temple is composed of Jews and Gentiles. It is the fruit of the redemption worked by Jesus.

What about the glory of the church?

> ...through the church the manifold wisdom
> of God might now be made known to the
> rulers and authorities in the heavenly places
> (Eph. 3:10).

We are the trophy of God's wisdom to the angels and rulers in the heavenly places. That means we are being watched. Paul goes so far as to say that the members of the church will judge angels (1 Cor. 6:1–2).

What about the status of the church in future glory?

> ...to him be glory in the church and in Christ
> Jesus throughout all generations, forever and
> ever. Amen (Eph. 3:21)

The glorification of God is tied to Christ *and* the church! God is magnified not just in the person of his Son, but in the body of Christ. This is a remarkable statement.

Here is how the church works out its life:

> And he gave the Apostles, the prophets, the evangelists, the pastors and teachers, to equip the saints for the work of ministry, for building up the body of Christ, until we all attain to the unity of the faith and of the knowledge of the Son of God, to mature manhood, to the measure of the stature of the fullness of Christ. (Eph. 4:11–13)

The gifts of the Spirit are given to the church so that the members of the body may come to maturity. More than that, the body itself comes to maturity in the fullness of Christ.

> Rather, speaking the truth in love, we are to grow up in every way into him who is the head, into Christ, from whom the whole body, joined and held together by every joint with which it is equipped, when each part is working properly, makes the body grow so that it builds itself up in love. (Eph. 4:15–16).

Paul picks up the imagery of a body and speaks of the church members engaging in multiple acts of mutual service. Christ, the head of the church, supplies nourishment to his body through the working of each member! There are so many "one-another's" in the New Testament. A short list would include these: forgive, forbear, encourage, stimulate to love and good works, love, live in harmony with, and do not pass judgment. The church is believers engaging with each other's lives. Relationships are the primary conduit for the flow of Christ's grace to the local church.

The goal is sanctification. Christ, the head of the church, ministers his grace through the gifted members of the body. The members grow to maturity and the church as a whole increases with godly increase. All this is done in a climate that embraces reality, faces it with humility, and runs to the cross as an antidote for all sin.

> Husbands, love your wives, as Christ loved the church and gave himself up for her, that he might sanctify her, having cleansed her by the washing of water with the word, so that he might present the church to himself in splendor, without spot or wrinkle or any such thing, that she might be holy and without blemish. (Eph. 5:25-27).

To summarize: the purpose of Jesus in his incarnation, death, and resurrection was to die for the church, to purchase a people of his own. His death will accomplish the cleansing of his bride until he presents her faultless in her final glory. It does not say that he will present individuals only. He will present the entire bride, all at once.

What does this have to do with us? My experience tells me that some pastors and a few laity have a picture of the church as the church. Most are indifferent to how the body is supposed to function. Their attitude to matters of government and discipline is pragmatic: whatever works. The point is this: local churches are to look like this: a new people, a corporate identity as a body, with all members functioning.

Some will say that Paul is talking about some abstract universal church – the invisible church. Absolutely not. These are not theoretical letters. They are written to local assemblies and their truth is to be applied to those assemblies. The church knows no abstraction. Local churches are the visible manifestations of the true body of Christ. The angels look down into existing, functioning churches and they are to see the wisdom of God. The work of pastors and teachers, Apostles and prophets is to be worked out in the ministry of every member to the local church, building itself up in love.

Here is how I picture this. There are certain geographical regions of the world where large stretches of dirt and forest are interrupted by massive formations of rock. These rocks seem to have pushed their way out through the soil and into the daylight. Usually these rocks are simply portions of massive rock layers beneath the surface. They are outcroppings. So it is with local churches. The real church, made up of all who are truly in Christ, rests just below the surface of our sight. However, it bursts forth in local assemblies, which represent the massive reality as yet unseen.

That means a local church is to look like these pictures in the New Testament. What she shall be in her full radiance is the manifestation of her present invisible reality. Someday the church will be seen. There will be unity across human barriers, godly relationships, ministry to each other with the gifts God has given – and Christ will be seen in his glory with his bride.

However, this is not theory. The outcroppings take their identity from this. We look to the future and seek to work that into our life now. It is real. It is true. It is why Spurgeon called a local church the "dearest place on earth."

This approach is necessary for two reasons. We must not define our churches based on sociology or cynicism.

First, the church is not defined sociologically. Sociology is the study of human society, how people function as a group, as a community, or as a nation. It has a place in understanding the dynamics of a church, its members, and their culture. It is a window. However, we do not determine what the church is to be by doing demographic studies.

As far as I can see the Apostles never did. They had plenty of opportunity to do so. The Roman world was rich with social castes, free and slave populations, languages and culture – all had been assimilated into the Roman Empire. It was cosmopolitan.

The church was formed in local assemblies in dozens of cities of the Mediterranean. It was made up of diverse people. Yes, the Apostles do not seem to focus on those "roots" as the source of a churches identity. They address the churches as "in Christ, in Corinth or whatever earthly locale may have been true". They are alien people, living on earth, at the end of the old age.

When they faced problems, the Apostles described what Christ died to accomplish in the church and what she will be one day and then exhorted the saints to work that out now. They did not say, "Look around. What kind of people do you want to reach? Define your reality by your target group. Adapt to the culture."

They were composed of all classes and genders, Jews and Gentiles. As a result, they had many differences and conflicts. The Apostles did not say, "Look at your demographics. Separate into homogeneous units. Jews with Jews, Gentiles with Gentiles." Such thinking turns the church into a club. No, the Apostles were called to work out their real unity in love and forbearance, humility and servanthood.

I have friends who are in Sri Lanka, a country torn by almost two decades of civil war between the Tamils and the Singhalese peoples. Hundreds have been murdered and imprisoned. These races hate each other everywhere – except in the church. They are the new community in Christ, the new race of humanity redeemed from sin.

Modern church growth specialists are counseling churches to make sociological adaptations. People are becoming increasingly self-defined and rigid. Music styles, dress codes, and worship formats are increasingly targeted to subgroups within the culture. The results are conflict, demands, selfishness, and divisions. I have witnessed a number of these targeted churches as they came to maturity. They reap what they sow. Their children become equally demanding. The parents remain as rigid as ever. While there is a place for sociology, it is limited. It robs churches of opportunity to show off the power of Christ.

I do not see any place in the New Testament for targeting homogeneous groups. No, the Apostles call the saints to live out today what will be their future glory.

The most dramatic example of this is 1 Corinthians 6. The Corinthian church had conflict between its members. There seem to have been some fraudulent business dealings and loss of money through this. Reacting as any pagan would, they sued each other in court, seeking redress for the wrongs done. So what can be wrong with this? Listen to Paul. I will quote the entire passage and highlight the arguments that show the apostolic appeal to future glory as a basis for present action.

> When one of you has a grievance against another, does he dare go to law before *the unrighteous* instead of *the saints*? Or do you not know that the *saints will judge the world*? And if the *world is to be judged by you*, are you incompetent to try *trivial cases*? Do you not know that we are to *judge angels*? How much more, then, *matters pertaining to this life*! So if you have such cases, why do you lay them before those who have *no standing in the church*? I say this to *your shame. Can it be* that there is no one among you wise enough to settle a dispute between *the brothers*, but *brother goes to law against brother*, and that before *unbelievers*?
> (1 Cor. 6:1–6, ESV).

There is nothing vague about this. Their future identity is to control their present actions. They should be ashamed of their loss of identity. Believers and unbelievers will have nothing in common then. Saints will hold positions of deep glory and authority. Angels will be beneath us. That being the case, can't the Corinthians work out their disputes in the resources of Christ already at work in them? Paul expects the church to work out its relational difficulties in light of her identity in Christ, not her identity in Corinth.

Now we arrive at the second concern: cynicism. I can hear the weak and doubting saint, worn by years of reality in the church, say, "Yes, that all sounds good in theory, but we know it does not work that way. Let's be practical."

This may sound like pragmatism. In reality I have found it to be the response of those who tried to live by the biblical model and met with stiff resistance. They retreat. They settle down into low expectations.

While I understand the painful experiences that lead to this I reject the portrait of Scripture as impractical and of Paul as some kind of idealist. We need not abandon hope. Paul held forth this picture of the church to the happy Philippians and the troubled Corinthians. God's Word is his wisdom and can be worked out wonderfully. But reality is hard. This means we must always refer to the standard and not lose heart.

The conclusion is this: the church is glorious. That may be a position of faith, as she does not appear to be glorious. Moreover, the average member cares not in the least that this is so. The average pastor is worn down by the relentless weight of low expectations. It can be a taste of so much more. There can be life-changing, honest, biblical fellowship. It is such working of the body that is our hope for ministry in this decaying era.

Let us pursue this glory in practice. Let us seek to taste some of what will be our full inheritance in the coming age. Let us be the body of Christ. This is the truth and it works. A body seeking to function by gifts, in mutual ministry, working out their glorious identity in the present works: this kind of church can be very effective. It changes lives, but it is not paradise! Let us resist low and feeble ideas of the church. This is how Matthew 18 will work.

Let's explore for a minute a little more of what biblical fellowship is all about. A family friend of many years said she went to church to hear a sermon that gave her meaning for her week. When her pastor asked her what he should preach about, she said, "Preach about the Bible and preach about twenty minutes.' This woman had an identity crisis.

I think of many folks like her who "go to church" on Sunday and go home. That is not the church. They have no sense of the role of pastors as overseers of their souls. They would never go to a pastor for counsel with a troubled conscience or help in a besetting sin. Even if they considered that as possible, they would never consider sharing their life with another believer. Their relationships with fellow members are social.

Here is what that looks like. Conversations on Sunday are about work, investments, the sports teams, their golf game, and their kids. A crisis of health may be shared and people may rally around at such a time. This is good. Some do not share even that. Words like these are rarely heard: "How may I pray for you this week John?" "How have you seen God at work in your life this week?" "Would you pray for me and hold me accountable in the area of my temper. I have been really harsh with the kids lately." "Would you pray with me for a co-worker who is not yet a Christian but open to the Gospel?" "Mary, you have such a gift of mercy. I want to encourage you to use it as fully as possible." Indeed, many would consider this type of conversation intrusive. I am not speaking here of liberal churches, but of evangelical ones. The members and pastors co-exist as marbles in a jar, touching each others lives only peripherally.

This is not biblical fellowship. There is no mutual confession, encouragement, prayer, love, burden-bearing, forbearance, forgiveness, compassion, speaking truth, using words that build up. In such fellowship the conversation is safe and happy, and people leave it feeling good but not edified or strengthened in the faith.

Such churches are lacking an adequate circulatory system. The large arteries are present, from pastor to people, but the capillaries which do the work of delivering the nutrition to the cells are absent. The cells are malnourished and weak. "Speaking the truth in love" calls for the members to talk truth with each other, truth taught by the gifted men.

I am fairly convinced that the primary barrier to real fellowship (where the members of a local church experience the work of the Spirit in their lives, building them up in Christ) is pride. We do not want to walk in the light with each other because it will ruin our image. It is scary to let people into our lives and allow them to expose our faults. If we do not, we shall not be the church. We shall be a club.

I know the power of these things. I was converted just as I headed off to the University. My earliest days as a Christian were rich. Our campus fellowship taught us to study Scripture. We did so a great deal. We prayed many days a week. We attended a local church nearby and sang the roof off. We served each other and exhorted each other.

I remember a few things about those early days. One was a brother in Christ who spent time getting to know me. Then one day he graciously took me aside and, using Scripture, pointed out some major faults. He did so because I was offending non-believers in my sin. He did not want me to dishonor the Gospel. This strikes me because it is one of a few times in my life where someone did that. Most of them took place in those early years.

I benefited greatly from this admonition. I grew because of it. I wish others did the same.

I also remember our conversations. We talked about the Bible and we talked about our lives. We talked about how to apply the Bible. We prayed for each other and with each other. One older student went to lunch with me three days a week, just to encourage me.

Recently I have pursued a friend in Christ with whom I meet weekly. We pray with each other and we openly talk about the Bible and how it applies to our lives, and we confess our sin. It is rich to have one who knows me, warts and all, and calls me to be godly with patience.

This strikes me because I have been in churches where talking about the Lord and his work in our lives was very rare. However, this is what the church is to be about.

It is at these crucial points that the church must be pursuing God's plan if she is to have any redemptive effect in the world of the lost and with the lives of saints who wage war against sin each day. It is in these relationships as a body, in the personal and risky sharing of life and heart under the Gospel, where we meet with the work of the Spirit in sanctification.

When a church moves toward this expression of being the body of Christ, the effects are astounding. Lives are changed. Reality overcomes pretense. Humility grows and pride is put to death.

The church is not ours to make into what we wish. She is Christ's. Her purpose, her function, her gifts are determined by him. The church, empowered by the Spirit, is transforming. Pastors must faithfully minister the Gospel and engage with people's lives as physicians of the soul. Members must merge their lives in covenant and love and mutual encouragement in the pursuit of holiness. This is our role in our dying cultures – to be outposts of the heavenly people of God in the midst of the inhabitants of the earth. We are to be a taste of the kingdom.

This will never be done perfectly. Yet we must measure ourselves by the right standard. Let's get out our Bibles and draw a picture of a healthy body of believers. Then let's pursue it with humility, prayer, dependence upon the Spirit, and persistence.

2

The Lord's Church

On the whole, I do not find Christians, outside the
catacombs, sufficiently sensible of the conditions.
Does anyone have the foggiest idea what sort of
power we so blithely invoke? The churches are
children playing on the floor with their chemistry
sets, mixing up a batch of TNT to kill a Sunday
morning. It is madness to wear ladies' velvet hats
to church; we should all be wearing crash helmets.
Ushers should issue life preservers and signal
flares; they should lash us to our pews. For the
sleeping god may wake some day and take offense.
                                            Annie Dillard

* * * * *

I have a friend who was among the elite company of
NASA's "teacher in space" program. He was one of
two from the State of Arizona. That program came
to an end with the Space shuttle Challenger tragedy
in 1986.

Such an honor required an extensive training and conditioning. Part of that training was developing skills in fielding questions from a press corps. One of the techniques offered was called "bridging." Bridging is what one does when the questioner asks a question which cannot be answered without violating security or confidentiality. It is simple: Don't answer the question. Turn the focus to less important issues. Answer by focusing them on something else. "So you want to know about the optical resolution of orbiting satellites? Well, the weather was clear in Boston last year. Next question."

The devil has mastered this technique by a factor of 100. The history of the church tells of his ability to take key texts and turn them on their head so we focus on the peripheral, not the central. Matthew 16 is such a passage.

> And I tell you, you are Peter, and on this rock I will build my church, and the gates of hell shall not prevail against it. I will give you the keys of the kingdom of heaven, and whatever you bind on earth shall be bound in heaven, and whatever you loose on earth shall be loosed in heaven. (Matt. 16:18–19).

Endless debates on "who is the Rock on which Christ builds?" have kept us from the beauty of the passage. We have considered the nature of the church in the purpose of God. We are the new human race. Now we turn to the ownership of the church and clarify her mission. This defines her boundaries. This passage also speaks to the enemy with whom we engage.

The Lord of glory, anticipating his imminent death and resurrection, tells his disciples that he will build his church and the gates of hell shall not prevail against it. Here we have the church, the people of God, promised by the Son of God! His purpose is to create his people. Note that this is an invincible purpose. The Son of God has set himself to this task and it will be done. He also notes that he gives to the church the authority to function within his purposes. It is authority but it is limited. We will look at more on this later.

He accomplishes this building of the church by his death and resurrection, of which he speaks in the verses which follow.

> From that time Jesus began to show his disciples that he must go to Jerusalem and suffer many things from the elders and chief priests and scribes, and be killed, and on the third day be raised. (Matt. 16:21).

It is the Lord's church. He says "my" church and he is the builder. He has laid down his life to purchase his people from every kindred and tribe and nation. He gave himself to rescue them from sin and to make them zealous of good works. He clarifies the nature of her war. He employs an unusual image.

The debate which follows, between Jesus and Peter, shows the nature of the church. Flesh and blood perspectives are anathema to Jesus. The church is counter-cultural. Suffering precedes glory. It is a community of those who abandon themselves for the purpose of Christ. It is a gathering of those who live for eternal life.

> And Peter took him aside and began to rebuke him, saying, "Far be it from you, Lord! This shall never happen to you." But he turned and said to Peter, "Get behind me, Satan! You are a hindrance to me. For you are not setting your mind on the things of God, but on the things of man." Then Jesus told his disciples, "If anyone would come after me, let him deny himself and take up his cross and follow me. For whoever would save his life will lose it, but whoever loses his life for my sake will find it. For what will it profit a man if he gains the whole world and forfeits his life? Or what shall a man give in return for his life? (Matt. 16:22–6).

Let's take this apart in more detail. Jesus addresses the purpose of the church and its enemy early on. The church is in a direct confrontation with the gates of hell. They do not prevail against her. How do gates not prevail? Gates are defensive. Prevailing is an offensive term. The gates of hell are obviously a picture of Satan's kingdom boundaries.

What is the rule of Satan? It is a rule that seeks the eternal destruction of men and women. It is a rule that does so by deceiving, and enticing into sin and judgment. Satan is a murderer and a liar.

Behind this imagery are the aggressive posture of the church and the violent response of the empire of hell. If I might paraphrase the whole thought, "I will build my church, the very building of it will be a frontal assault on the rule of Satan, de-populating his kingdom, and his defenses will fall before me." The point is the ownership and mission of the church.

The church is an alien race, citizens of another country, inhabiting a foreign plant. Our purpose, our rule, our life together is distinct. This defines the WHY of church discipline. We cherish holiness and see sin as an enemy. We would sacrifice anything to be holy.

Our society will not. She is preoccupied with other priorities and prepared to compromise a little integrity for the same of profitability. We function out of rhythm with the society in which we live because we are a holy people in a crooked and perverse generation. Jesus owns us. Church discipline is part of the expression of the assault on the rule of the evil one.

The church is the creation of the Lord Christ for all eternity. As we have seen. The rest of the New Testament expands on this: we are the bride, the new humanity in the new Adam, the new man created of people of all races, the new temple. We are aliens, a distinct people, and a colony of heaven on earth. Jesus does not call us to improve the world, but to bring the Gospel to the world. Let's get to more specifics.

First, this tells us what we are not supposed to do. The war the church engages in is not a war to take over society or to apply biblical standards to the country in which we live. The kingdom of God manifested in the church is spread through every culture, as a counter-culture. It is spiritual, not territorial. Any identification of the kingdom with a particular country or form of government is a gross distortion of the purpose of the church and the nature of Christ's people.

I live in a country where many of the Christians think we are a unique people, that America is somehow a form of the kingdom of God and enjoys the special favor of God. We do a great deal of lamenting the loss of our Christian America. We put forth a great deal of energy in seeking to recover our Christian past. We constantly judge the world and its practices. We seek to reform society and bring it "back to God."

While it is good and right for Christians to be participants in society, to serve in its government, to seek just and wise laws for the good of all citizens, it is not within our authority to seek to create an earthly kingdom for Christ. Nor will it work.

The Puritan experiment in New England is proof of this. Citizenship in the kingdom of Christ cannot be inherited or passed on to the next generation. Each person is born of the Spirit. Whatever may have been the aspirations of the founding fathers of a country like America, they were in error. No earthly nation may claim to be a representation of the kingdom of God. This leads to arrogance and an inability to analyze ourselves.

Paul directs the Corinthians away from judging the citizens of this world and tells them they are not to be isolated from life and sinners. He points them in an entirely different direction.

Listen to his statement of this, as he narrows the scope of the church's responsibility for itself, and keeps them from a wrong mission to the world:

> I wrote to you in my letter not to associate with sexually immoral people – not at all meaning the sexually immoral of this world, or the greedy and swindlers, or idolaters, since then you would need to go out of the world. But now I am writing to you not to associate with anyone who bears the name of brother if he is guilty of sexual immorality or greed, or is an idolater, reviler, drunkard, or swindler- not even to eat with such a one. For what have I to do with judging outsiders? Is it not those inside the church whom you are to judge? (1 Cor. 5:9–12).

While we will explore this section later, it is essential to see that he is assuming that the church is a separate kingdom. We are a colony of expatriates operating with our own rules and government. It is not our business to judge the world. So what is the church to do?

Second, it tells us what we are to do and how we are to live. We are to lay siege to the gates of hell with the Gospel. Our combat is spiritual, not physical. The church engages in a holy war with the principalities and powers. Her weapons are not of the flesh.

The rock on which Jesus builds his church would appear to be Peter's confessional position, the person of Jesus as Messiah and Savior. Jesus is the Gospel. The means of his accomplishment is his suffering, death, and resurrection. The attitude of his followers is of forsaking themselves for him. They live for eternal life and will not gain the whole world and lose their souls. A fleshly perspective is unwelcome. It is rebuked.

Filling in the details from the rest of the New Testament, we would find that the mission of the church and the authority she has received is to advance the Gospel against the kingdom of darkness. Jesus' purpose in his death defines our mission. That advance takes place in two spheres: evangelism and edification. The Gospel delivers people from the wrath to come, forms them into a people of his own, purifies them to be a distinct people in the present age, and assures them of ultimate deliverance from sin. Sin and Satan are the great enemies.

We must constantly reinforce the purpose of Jesus. If this is lost or abandoned, and other weapons are taken up, she steps out from her delegated authority and ceases to be the church. Let's break this down further.

First, the truth of the Gospel must be preserved. As we read the rest of the New Testament we find that apostolic zeal is at its peak when it comes to keeping the Gospel pure and central to the life of the church. Any distortion is corrected, and distortions there will be:

> But false prophets also arose among the people, just as there will be false teachers among you, who will secretly bring in destructive heresies, even denying the Master who bought them, bringing upon themselves swift destruction. And many will follow their sensuality, and because of them the way of truth will be blasphemed. And in their greed they will exploit you with false words.
> (2 Pet. 2:1–3).

The apostolic letters reveal that they labor at a Gospel perspective against false teachers.

Paul corrects the Colossians for thinking there is some merit to their rituals, angelic visions, and asceticism. He is particularly upset with the Galatians. He anathematizes their error. He is not just angry, he is right. What people believe, in what they trust, bears directly on their everlasting destiny. Any dilution of the fullness of Christ, and addition to the "zero" contribution of the believer changes everything.

Here are the simple implications, to be worked out in detail as we move forward with this study. First, the church must live out its commitment to the truth of the Gospel. However, there is need for wisdom here. Paul does not anathematize the Corinthians for doubting the resurrection (1 Cor. 15). He does not damn the Colossians for turning to mediators and mysticism in their spiritual growth (Col. 2:6–23). He corrects. Damning and correcting have a different tone. Both of them are rooted in the belief that the truth of the Gospel matters.

This means that there is a place for drawing a line and excluding those who deny the Gospel. Paul called churches to do just that, and expected that the Galatians would bring judgment upon their troublemakers. *The Evangelical Celebration*, published in recent years, is a grand step forward to clarifying our common convictions in the nature of salvation.

Yet we must be careful. We wield holy weapons with dirty hands. I have watched the defense of truth become ugly and divisive. A young man defended his Calvinism by taking a swing at an elder! Mature faculty members, with offices on the same floor of the same building, wrote books advocating different positions and criticized the other's works but never talked to each other! The most orthodox people of Jesus' day called for his crucifixion.

Second, the application of the Gospel must be constant. The Apostles also seek to bring the message of the Gospel to bear on every problem in the church and in the individual believer. Let me define that further. The letters of the New Testament speak to problems in the churches in a way remarkably different from how I do. I, and others, tend to be moralistic. We apply rules and laws to the church and ask them to straighten up. "Stop that. It's sin. Do this. It's a command."

However, this is not the apostolic method. They bring the life, death, burial, and resurrection of Jesus to bear on every situation. Few churches had more problems. Few letters are more indicative of this than 1 Corinthians. Here is a list of how Paul pursued Gospel application to their problems.

1. Their divisions were a repudiation of the Gospel in that they gloried and identified in what the Gospel judges: wisdom, wealth, gifts. Paul calls them to apply the world-judging Gospel to their disunity and to boast only in Christ (1 Cor. 1).

2. Their boasting in superior wisdom is refuted by pointing out that the kind of wisdom they glory in is the same wisdom that crucified the Lord of glory. Paul tells them that the wisdom of God is revealed by the Spirit and that wisdom is the cross (1 Cor. 2).

3. Their perspective on leaders and their elevation of them to the status of gurus is a denial of the humiliation and the glory of Christ and his role as the builder of the church and judge of all who work in this field. Their despising of the church is a despising of the temple of Christ. They need a right perspective on leaders. (1 Cor 4).

4. Their boasting in the freedom of a Christian by tolerating incestuous behavior is a denial of

their unique identity as the new people of God. They are to deal with sin, not co-operate with it, for this is what Christ died for. Their lawsuits are a repudiation of their glorious identity and future vocations as judges of the world. Their immorality is a contradiction to their union with Christ and the intent of his death (1 Cor 5–6)

5. In Corinth, there was a growing detachment from physical reality. They exaggerated the doctrine of the new creation. This manifested itself in bizarre attitudes toward marriage and sexuality. Paul corrects this by pointing out that the world to come is not yet and they should live in purity, for which marriage was given (1 Cor. 7).

6. Freedom and pride were mixed in Corinth, each believer boasting in their understanding of the new age Christ had inaugurated. It led them to an assertion of their rights in freedom. They offended their brothers and sisters who had not yet come to their understanding of freedom. Paul calls them to the love and servanthood of true followers of Christ (1 Cor. 8–10)

7. The abuses of the Lord's Supper were corrected. Paul rebukes the divisions by economic class at the Lord's Supper. He notes that the church gathers as "one body" in Christ. Their behavior violated the meaning of Jesus' death. (1 Cor. 11).

8. Spiritual gifts were being used for self aggrandizement and not for service. Paul calls them to be a body, to serve each other, to put the good of the whole ahead of personal good. This is working out the Gospel in the life of a church, so that it is not a collection of marbles in a jar, but a true new community (1 Cor 12–14).

9. The doctrine of the resurrection, being denied in Corinth as part of their repudiation of the "flesh," is reasserted. Their salvation is tied inseparably to their physical being just as Jesus' was (1 Cor. 15).

In every case Paul applies the Gospel to the life of the church. He does not speak of morality only. He does not tell them simply to "stop doing that." He works out the meaning of the death, burial, and resurrection of Christ as it speaks to every issue.

We must keep the Gospel in the center. If we lose the Gospel, we lose everything. Every sermon and every time of worship in song should take us back to the cross and its broad meaning for all: the non-believer and the believer.

Third, the Gospel itself is a message which disciplines. This is how Paul describes the grace of God in Titus 2.

> For the grace of God has appeared, bringing salvation for all people, training us to renounce ungodliness and worldly passions,

and to live self-controlled, upright, and godly
lives in the present age . . . (Titus 2:11–12).

Here the word translated "training us" is the
word for "training children by discipline"
(*paideûo*). Grace disciplines!

Jesus died and rose again to make the church
holy. Years ago I was surprised to see that the major
passages which speak of the purpose of Christ's
death focus on more than forgiveness. They are
usually larger in scope: to make us holy, to bring
us to God. And they are most often in the plural.
Jesus died to make a people of his own.

The Gospel guards against idealistic demands
because it insists we are sinners. If we become
perfectionists in our expectations, people will be
treated either with severity or they will knuckle
under and fake it. Churches where there is no
freedom to acknowledge sin or failure are gross
distortions of the redemptive bodies of the New
Testament. If God's people, struggling with
remaining sin or the weakness of the body, are not
free to get help in their local fellowship, where will
they go?

The Gospel guards against trying harder by
insisting we are powerless to be holy. I have seen
moralism creep into the church. This leads to a
pharisaical pride in a form of righteousness that
has more to do with cultural taboos than with heart
holiness: people who think God is pleased with their
driving old cars, wearing drab clothes, not using
technology, and abstaining from alcohol or dancing

with their wife, such people have substituted a worldly religion for the glorious Gospel. Paul called such practices a form of paganism in Galatians 4:8–11! I believe the greatest enemy of the Gospel is morality and religious activity. The self-righteous and pious are the ones who killed Jesus.

The holiness we seek to engender in the Spirit is the work of the New Covenant. It is the writing of the law on the heart by the Spirit and involves an internal submissiveness and softness of heart to God, a compassion for others, and the control of tongue and passions in obedience. When sin breaks out in the life of a member of the community, it is a mark of their sickness, and the people and leaders must act to treat the disease according to Christ. We do this with humility, as personally and protectively as possible, and only severely when all else fails.

Finally, we apply the Gospel by keeping love and unity in the church. Sins against love do matter. Division is a violation of the Gospel. Most of these have to do with gossip, slander, and a critical or judgmental spirit. The Apostles sought to stir the love of the church into a white-hot conflagration, where love covers personal offenses. In such white-hot love, the stumbling of others is covered and their shame is not exposed. Jesus did say that love is the one standard by which the world judges the church (John 13:33–5). Sometimes people defend the truth in ugly ways. Some of the worst dogfights I have ever seen in churches were between people of strong commitment to truth. One man insisted to me that anyone who did not believe in twenty-four hour days in creation could not be a Christian, and he frequently wrote angry letters to any who did not take his position.

The middle years of the twentieth century saw a number of major denominations labor against the infiltration of Gospel-denying theology. At times, this battle was fought with patience and grace. In other cases, a critical and fighting spirit developed. Many abandoned the faith in the face of such detestable pride and acrimony in Christian leaders.

One of those was Dr. Francis Schaeffer. As a result of the bitter disputes he saw, he faced a time of despair. He saw the ugliness of churches fighting over truth when ego took hold. He came back to Scripture and concluded that Christians should value truth *and* love. When we disagree we must do it differently than the world. The mark of the Christian is love.

Unity is rooted in truth, but relationships are the place it works out. Humility and forbearance are crucial to sustaining unity. All of this is an application of Gospel truth. As Paul says, "Here (in the local church) there can be neither Jew nor Gentile, circumcised or uncircumcised, barbarian, Scythian, slave or free, but Christ is all and in all" (Col. 1:11).

The Gospel, applied to the life of the believer and the local church is a working out of the purpose of Christ to build his people. It assures us that the gates of hell will not prevail as we faithfully apply the message of Jesus to all situations, denying ourselves and serving him as we do so.

3

The Blemished Bride

The churches of the Revelation show us that churches are not Victorian parlors where everything is always picked up and ready for guests. They are messy family rooms. Entering a person's house unexpectedly, we are sometimes met with a barrage of apologies. St. John does not apologize. Things are out of order, to be sure, but that is what happens to churches that are lived in. They are not show rooms. They are living rooms, and if the persons living in them are sinners, there are going to be clothes scattered about, handprints on the woodwork, and mud on the carpet.

Eugene Peterson

* * * * *

So the church is glorious is it? Our mission is to lay siege to the kingdom of Satan with the Gospel? Some may respond to this with a shrug of the shoulders. If my teenage children heard this, they might encourage me to take a "reality pill." As pastor's kids, they have witnessed ugly sin and cover-up in the life of the local church.

Some may hear this and become hard-nosed idealists. They dream of a church where things are the way they are supposed to be. They believe that strong leadership can make this kind of glory happen here and now. They criticize local bodies which do not measure up, sometimes harshly. I did.

I had always been an idealist. My neighbors called me the "little preacher." I loved to call people to morality. I criticized adults for their prejudices. I brought that baggage with me into the Christian life.

New in Christ, I baptized my idealism with Christian perspectives. The church would be the perfect place I hoped for. I composed my model from scraps and portions of the New Testament combined with tidbits of utopia. My favorite book was Acts. My favorite passage was Acts 2:42–7.

> And they devoted themselves to the Apostles' teaching and fellowship, to the breaking of bread and the prayers. And awe came upon every soul, and many wonders and signs were being done through the Apostles. And all who believed were together and had all things in common. And they were selling their possessions and belongings and distributing the proceeds to all, as any had need. And day by day, attending the temple together and

breaking bread in their homes, they received their food with glad and generous hearts, praising God and having favor with all the people. And the Lord added to their number day by day those who were being saved.

Here was a church worth attending. Such brilliant spirituality! Conversions occurred every day. They did it right! I thought this is what the church would be.

All was well until I ran into the real thing. I became part of a local church. People were not passionate about prayer. They avoided other believers with whom they had differences. They skipped out on the Lord's Supper. They held onto their money when others had need. This was not impressive. In place of shouting praise, there was the reading of the bulletin. Where deep unity should reign there was criticism of carpet colors. Like many, I battled with disillusionment. How can I believe the glory of the church is real and then be part of this kind of assembly?

Once I was a Christian, it took years to get over the shock of what the church was really like. Many times, I was tempted to head to the mission field where I was certain these problems did not exist. I moved into the parachurch work to get away from the ugliness of the church. Even there I stumbled over ugly reality. Then I tried Christian education. Surely a seminary would be sub-specie of my ideal kingdom of God? Not at all. I was being tempted to find a perfect church or perfect Christian community – or at least one worthy of my attention.

As I sorted this out with a Bible and true comrades in the faith, I came to understand what great theologians called the "now" and the "not yet." We have future glory now, in part, but the old order of sin still lingers. This was the nature of life in a congregation, a glorious body of Christ.

One of the passages that helped me most was Colossians 3:1–17. I quote verses 1–6 here.

> If then you have been raised with Christ, seek the things that are above, where Christ is, seated at the right hand of God. Set your minds on things that are above, not on things that are on earth. For you have died, and your life is hidden with Christ in God. When Christ who is your life appears, then you also will appear with him in glory. Put to death therefore what is earthly in you: sexual immorality, impurity, passion, evil desire, and covetousness, which is idolatry. On account of these the wrath of God is coming.

Paul describes the invisible reality of the church. He assures the church in Colosse that reality is in Christ. However, it is invisible for now. He tells this church, battling with error, that they will be seen in glory some day. In light of that they are to put sin to death.

Sin is still among them. Their real glory is not inconsistent with present sin. It is because of their "in Christ" relationship that they are able to put sin to death. There must have been immorality, impurity, covetousness in the church or Paul would

not have called them to put these to death. Paul
expands on this further in verses 9–14:

> Do not lie to one another, seeing that you have
> put off the old self with its practices and have
> put on the new self, which is being renewed
> in knowledge after the image of its creator.
> Here there is not Greek and Jew, circumcised
> and uncircumcised, barbarian, Scythian, slave,
> free; but Christ is all, and in all. Put on then,
> as God's chosen ones, holy and beloved,
> compassion, kindness, humility, meekness,
> and patience, bearing with one another and,
> if one has a complaint against another,
> forgiving each other; as the Lord has forgiven
> you, so you also must forgive. And above all
> these put on love, which binds everything
> together in perfect harmony.

Two things are apparent here. First, the glorious
unity of the body of Christ is now established as
the basis for the expression of that oneness in acts
of kindness and humility. Second, sin is present in
the church, or there would be no reason for
forgiveness. Saints are flawed or there is no reason
for forbearance. Divisions are real or there is
no need to be reminded of the significance of
Christ.

From this and other passages, I came to this
conclusion. This glory of the church was being
worked out in the trenches of human wrongdoing.
Believers were still drawn into transgression by the
power of indwelling sin. Gatherings of believers

were made up of such folk. They, too, faced the realities of sin. I embraced what I call a realistic holiness. The bar is raised to the appropriate level, the measure of God's law. As a result, church is faced for what it is.

There are too many examples that clarify this. Here is one. One Sunday, we had a particularly happy and wondrous time in worship. People sang heartily. Some closed their eyes. A few raised their hands. There was an anointing on my preaching, and an attentive response from the congregation. People rose from worship and the room was filled with life.

One of the members approached me. She was beaming, encouraged from the time of worship in song and Scripture study. "Pastor that was a wonderful service. God really met with us," they commented. I was encouraged. They explained how the Scripture had spoken to them, then, pulling me aside, they said, "Did you hear that Mr. X is very upset about the new chairs in the sanctuary. He thinks their color is irreverent." I was taken back. Here was gossip, indirect communication, and nonsense all wrapped into one sentence. Here are glory and squalor together.

It was as if someone decorated their house in gold and cheap plastic. Here were glorious life transformations. Here was hypocrisy, stubborn-heartedness, racism, and reluctant witnesses that had to be kicked out of the nest.

This is the church. The Apostles wrote letters to problems, some more extreme than others, but problems nonetheless. Immorality, denial of the Gospel, pursuit of angelic mediation, boasting in specialized knowledge available only to the select few, divisions, interpersonal conflicts, and desecration of the Lord's Supper: the list of evils only begins here. Of the seven churches of Revelation only two receive commendations; the other five hear admonitions, some severe. Moral, theological, and spiritual problems persist. No church is perfectly healthy.

So, do we give up hope and abandon the local assembly? Do we lower our expectations?

I have a friend who suffered terribly in his church. One ecclesiastical trial followed another. He was accused of heresy, of leading the church into compromise. His name was slandered. At last, he quit. He took his family and moved to a remote part of the United States where they could live alone and with little money. He remained there for more than a year.

One day a good friend called, having heard of his decisions. He knew the man was in great pain. He probed and drew out of him an hour's worth of lamentation. At the end of this time, he stated his conclusion to his compassionate listener, "I will never have anything to do with the church." There was a long pause. Finally, the reply came, "That's the stupidest thing I have ever heard."

Not in this age will the church cease to be anything other than mixed. A great novelist, Flannery O'Connor, addressed this years ago:

> All your dissatisfactions with the Church seem
> to me to come from an incomplete under-
> standing of sin ... What you seem to demand
> is that the Church put the kingdom of heaven
> on earth right now and here – that the Holy
> Ghost be translated at once into all flesh. The
> Holy Spirit rarely shows Himself on the
> surface of anything. To have the Church be
> what you want it to be would require the
> continuous miraculous meddling of God in
> human affairs, whereas it is to retain our
> dignity that God has chosen to operate in
> another manner. We can't reject that without
> rejecting life ... Christianity makes a difference;
> but it cannot kill the age. [1]

We are called to seek the standard of purity and
love called for by the Gospel. Nevertheless, the
expectation is not harsh, demanding, and cruel. It
is realistic. Jesus' purpose in his death will prevail,
but in this era we labor to put sin to death and put
on Christ. In this mortal body we groan. We were
saved in hope and that hope is not yet realized.
The church has glory and squalor in its present
state. We pursue the glory, abhor the squalor, but
not with tyranny or perfectionist idealism. Yet we
ask, how?

There are some who think the way to deal with
this is for the church to become a doctrine and
teaching center. Great instruction loaded up into
the brains of the saints gives them all they need to

1. Cited on p.42, *Reversed Thunder* by Eugene Paterson, San
Francisco, Harper San Francisco, 1988

progress in godliness. Each believer leaves church on Sunday and works out their salvation by themselves. They practice the spiritual disciplines and apply the Word to their lives.

The flaw in this is that we are all blind to ourselves. We cannot make it alone. Moreover, the church is not an educational institution.

A contrasting method is a heavy focus on shepherding, where the elders are deeply involved in the lives of the members. Only the mature are allowed to join. Everyone is under oversight and told to submit to the leaders. In some cases, their every decision is under scrutiny. Rigid programs and rules are imposed and saints live under the heavy yoke of busybody oversight.

However, Jesus did not tell the Apostles to set higher and higher entrance requirements to combat reality. This was the heresy of the later Donatists. It is a form of man-made religion; a self-reliance of trying harder that actually denies the Gospel. There are churches today that create such an elevated standard for taking communion that few actually enjoy this reminder of mercy. A feast of grace becomes a place of discouragement to stumbling sinners who are honest enough to admit their sin.

Tertullian noted that Jesus was crucified between two thieves: immorality and religion. While we do not consider moral people to be enemies of the faith, they were the ones who crucified Jesus.

Moralists are people who confuse the Gospel with morality. They think that people are really changed by being told how to behave. They believe the ministry of the church is with a wagging finger, chiding people for their sins. They have changed Christianity into a religion, a list of do's and don'ts and simplistic solutions to life's problems. They find their hope in getting rid of the mess of life by defining it away. Life is not messy, they say. Just read your Bible, pray every day, go to church, and prayer meetings, don't go to theater, don't spend time with the dirty, and all will be well.

Church leadership and Christian fellowship must shun all self-righteousness. Our attitude to each other must be one of bearing gently with the ignorance and errors of others because we know these are our own burden as well. Some may think that tongue lashings and heavy guilt are the way to motivate. Pastors and fellow believers may speak in the tone of voice of a Master Sergeant berating his trainees at boot camp. "What's wrong with you? You're lazy. You call yourself a man. My dog has more courage than you do."

None of these is honoring to the Gospel. The passage we are considering is Jesus' method for dealing with sin in the midst of the church.

We have lived in a variety of homes throughout our marriage. Most of them have had a garden in the back. I love the beauty of a garden. Cool summer evenings in the garden area are a great pleasure. Anticipating our summer enjoyments, every spring we dug up the soil, planted the flowers, and reseeded the lawn.

However, reality set in. Weeds grew. They took

over the flower beds. There was only one solution. We had to go outside and pull the weeds. We had to do so every week. Wherever there was a weed, we pulled it. So it is with the church. That is what Matthew 18 is about. "When your brother sins" is the equivalent of "when the weeds appear."

There is something that precedes Matthew 18 too. It is called self-judgment. I pull my own weeds. I take Scripture and apply it to my own life. The Holy Spirit convicts me. I confess and repent.

> But if we judged ourselves truly, we would not be judged. But when we are judged by the Lord, we are disciplined so that we may not be condemned along with the world.
> (1 Cor. 11:31–32).

If that is not effective, Jesus says we help each other. I cannot make it alone. I do not see myself accurately. I can deceive myself. Others are there to help me walk in the light.

Unless we begin here, we may become cruel tyrants of the churches we serve. Church discipline is not a whip. "Lording it over the flock" wears out the saints. The quest for purity must be exercised with the patience of Jesus. Church discipline is necessary. Real church discipline is daily. It takes place in conversation, confession, repentance, rebuke, and obedience.

Therefore, we must embrace the difficulties of church life. We must embrace the Gospel as the basis for our realism. There are no churches that are doctrinally perfect and morally complete. Nor will there be perfection until Jesus completes his work. He died for his bride that he might cleanse her and present her without blemish in the day of Christ. His grace is manifested to teach us to say no to ungodliness and to cause us to live godly lives now, to purify us for him. Someday he will present us faultless with great joy. Meanwhile we need the Gospel every day.

If we do not do this, we may try to paint ourselves as better than we are. Churches cannot be glitzy, well-oiled places and be real at the same time. Either we are sinners needing the Gospel, or we are self-righteous.

Look at the early church. If the early Christians were interested in making a good impression with the pagans, they failed miserably. They were, to use modern jargon, "real". Sin was present. Factions developed. Leaders failed and had arguments. Heresy developed. False teachers crept into and grew up within the church.

The glory we seek to show off as the new community of Christ is not artificial. It is not a marketing ploy. The glory of the church is worked out in the muck and mire of sanctification. It is not hanging our dirty laundry out to confess our failures and sins. We pursue holiness with transparent honesty about our present condition. Hypocrisy has no value in the kingdom of God.

Let me illustrate. I know of a church where their image became their passion. They desired to portray their togetherness to the community.

Everything they did was professional and sharp. They gloried in their problem-free lives. This concern with image became so strong that they decided that all matters of church discipline should be delegated to their Board, to be handled in a private way, so that no one would be embarrassed. When a new pastor sought to bring a matter to the whole church he was told that this was not their policy. He stood his ground. On another occasion he brought a sinning brother to the congregation for their correction. He was asked by those in leadership if this could be done another way next time. They found it embarrassing. It hurt their image in the community. A deadly fear of reality hung in the atmosphere.

On another note, there was a pastor named Ray Stedman. He pastored the Peninsula Bible Church in Palo Alto, California. God's Spirit visited them and a wave of conversions came. Ray was a very down-to-earth preacher. One night he was explaining the passage in 1 Corinthians 6. Here Paul describes the behavior of ungodly people in the city of Corinth. Then he highlights the wonder that the Corinthians were no longer these things. They had been washed, sanctified, and justified by the Lord Jesus Christ and the Spirit of God.

Spontaneously, Ray reread the list of sinners – thieves, drunkards, adulterers, and the like. He then asked people to stand if this was a good description of their life before they knew Christ. The vast majority of people stood. This heartened everyone. Some might find this shameful, a display of the dirty laundry of the fellowship. It was not so. After the service, a man approached Ray and said he was a visitor that night. He was not a Christian. He said he was amazed at the number of folks who stood. He concluded, "I have decided to come to this church because these are my kind of people." Reality was attractive to him. A phony image was not.

Pursuing holiness does not mean pretending to be holy. We are sinners who need the Gospel. Admitting our sin and facing it squarely is a deep reminder of our need of a Savior. This is appealing to the outsider and encouraging to the insider.

We must also see the reality of the church with hope in the Gospel. A friend once asked me to name the church in the New Testament I would least like to pastor. Corinth is the obvious choice. This church was filled with sin, heresy, division, and they were Paul's greatest critics. Then he asked me to study Paul's words about the Corinthians. Here is what I found:

1. He thanked God for them (1:4).
2. He affirmed their faith (1:5-6).
3. He noted the gifts of the Spirit to them (1:7)
4. He assured them that God would finish his work (1:8–9).
5. He praised them (11:2).
6. He called them brothers (15:1).
7. He loved them deeply (2 Cor. 2:4).
8. He boasted to Titus about them (2 Cor. 7:14).
9. He said he had complete confidence in them (2 Cor. 7:16).

That shocked me. Paul had not given up hope. He calls the church to judge herself. He calls her to judge sin in her midst. He calls her a church, a gathering of saints too. I had no reason to be in a judgmental posture. Paul saw this church through the new covenant, through Christ. We read in Ephesians that Jesus loved the church and gave himself for her, so that she will one day be without blemish (Ephesians 5:25–7). However, she was not perfect when he loved her! He loved her, warts and all. In addition, his grace will cleanse her and make her holy someday.

Here is the result for this book: this is first worked out in relationship. Discipline is expressed at every level, not as a mean-spirited harangue, but as the necessary corrective to sin and reminder of the Gospel call to holiness. Brothers and sisters in the body should function as comrades in a holy war, pursuing godliness. They should have agreement in the measure of holiness and they should apply it. First, they look at themselves and face reality. In addition, they tell a few friends of the war they face, their particular temptations, and their need of prayer. Then they help others apply it, in the context of humble and authentic fellowship in Christ.

My wife sat in a group of women not too long ago where this was the atmosphere. One of the women shared her sense of guilt in not getting all the things done that were before her each day. She was a mother of three young children. She lost her temper. She did not open her home to others as much as she wanted.

What struck my wife was how the other women helped her understand the standards of God, helped her get rid of false guilt, helped her see what the real sins were, and encouraged her to keep living under the cross. She came away heartened for the journey.

The function of the church is to build up, to encourage, to strengthen, to exhort, to support. We are to be friends in Christ who fan the flame of our faith and hope and love. This is where we begin.

4

For What Sins?

It is an illusion to think that you can just preach against sin and never do anything about it in the lives of the people and yet expect them to conform to the pattern of holiness.

John MacArthur

* * * * *

God sent his Son to redeem his people. He sent his Spirit to call and form them. We are an outpost of the kingdom of God on earth. We are to deal with sin but to do so with caution and wisdom, so as not to engage in holy war with dirty weapons. Jesus said that the first step in discipline is to go to your brother or sister in private. The condition for the whole process is this: "If your brother sins." What does that mean? What sins are worthy of the process of Matthew 18? Do we pursue this route for any and every sin?

Should there be church discipline for someone who is tempted to look aside by the immodest fashions of our day? Should there be discipline for the mother who occasionally yells at her kids in exasperation? What of the person who battles bitterness for terrible abuse suffered in childhood? When am I to admonish my brother? When do I step out and speak to my sister? If I start the process, is it inevitable that it be finished? Must all sin be brought to the church?

These are crucial questions. Missteps here could lead to a cult-like control of people's lives.

Let's go back to the nature of the church and the Gospel. One of the remarkable gifts of grace is that the penalty for sin has been paid. We no longer live under the threat that one transgression brings condemnation. In a certain sense, we have the freedom to grow. To put is as Paul says it, we are "learning what is pleasing to the Lord" (Eph. 5:10). James notes, "We all stumble in many ways" (Jam. 3:2). He is speaking of levels of maturity in the context of the growing self-control of those who mature in Christ.

This tells us that the church must be a place where people can grow, can begin as immature, and come to maturity. No matter where we draw the line of "when to speak to a brother" we must do so in a context of the Gospel and knowing that we all are maturing in Christ. Every day believers need the Gospel.

The new community is not a place where people are perfect. It is a place where people are honest about their sin. It is not a place of perfection, but of humility and the cross.

For What Sins?

The church is not a moral improvement society. It is a place where the Spirit of God is at work in professed believers. The Word of God and the Spirit of God work together to reveal areas for growth in godliness. We approach all matters in the context of faith in Christ's faithful work to his own. We are not anxious and worried as we face sin.

Moreover, no Christian is fully aware of his sins. I have witnessed churches where there is a great deal of pointing out of sin. It is done in the guise of hating sin and loving righteousness. Nevertheless, it is not according to the Gospel.

Paul even instructs the Philippians to walk according to the light they have. He notes that as they grow, there will be progressive clarity. Paul is patient.

> Let those of us who are mature think this way, and if in anything you think otherwise, God will reveal that also to you. Only let us hold true to what we have attained (Phil. 3:15–16).

At the same time, we can also see that our walk with Christ is not meant to be a "lone ranger" experience. There is a strong responsibility for each other.

Hebrews 3:12–13 is one of the most important passages for the maintenance of spiritual health in all of the New Testament.

> Take care, brothers, lest there be in any of you an evil, unbelieving heart, leading you to

fall away from the living God. But exhort one
another every day, as long as it is called
"today," that none of you may be hardened
by the deceitfulness of sin (ESV).

It speaks of the need to be encouraged daily, to
watch over each other's lives, to prevent hardening
in sin. There is real danger. We have blind spots.
We are not to try to make it alone.

A couple of things must be pointed out. First,
the ministry of Hebrews 3 is not the ministry of
pastors. That occurs in Hebrews 13:17. It is the
ministry of the members of the body to each other
in the close confines of a face-to-face relationship.
In that context we are known, we are observed,
we are loved. Because we are all inclined to self-
deception, it is all the more important to have those
around us who cut through our ability to pull the
wool over our own eyes.

I keep an eye on you and you keep an eye on
me, like good friends supporting each other. We
agree that sin is our great enemy. Sin is deceitful.
We are no match for it by ourselves. We ask the
other to help us fight sin. This is very hard to do.

Here is a first hint of when we are to speak to
our sinning brother or sister. It is when we see them
hardening their hearts. The ministry is one of
keeping an eye on each other, in a spirit of
encouragement. That means looking out for a
change of attitude, for a change of teachability, for
a change toward defensiveness. Here is the first
clue as to when we are to intervene in another's

life. The presence of another brother is light into my darkness. I need it for my own soul.

Over the years, I have observed that the worst cases of sin in the church have always been in believers who lived a life isolated from the intimacy of sharing the things of God with their brothers. No one knows them. They have no spiritual friends. I believe every believer needs a friend in Christ who knows them and watches over them. I also believe that believers need to be encouraged to go to their overseers when they face troubled consciences or habits of sin they cannot stop.

I have also seen many scandalous sins in the church. In every case I know people looked back and saw the signs that it was coming. They had considered saying something, but did not want to take the risk.

Let's take Bill. He was a member of the church where I was the pastor. He had a stellar reputation. As a result, no one thought it suspicious that Bill spent many lunches with another one of the members – a lady. They worked near each other. They had always been good friends.

They began to work as a committee of two planning some activities for their class at the church. This meant more time together. Everyone assumed the best. However, it went on for months. Then a full year went by. Bill began to change. He became defensive and angry. He resented long sermons. He began to criticize the church. She lost weight. Her doctors could not understand. None of us, including myself, thought anything of it.

It became too late. They were not innocently working together. They were involved in adultery. They had planned massive cover-up. Their lives were exhausted by duplicity.

The failure to intervene in another believer's life at the early stages of sin leads to a hardening of heart and more scandalous sins. A hardened heart is one that is calloused, unfeeling, and unresponsive to the Gospel. Daily encouragement prevents a callous from developing on the heart.

Any sin can become dominant. Any sin can be frequent. Any sin can be rationalized or become a hindrance to the believer's joy and obedience. We all have blind spots and we must watch out for each other.

I know this sounds intimidating. An entire generation has been trained to think that "all they need is Jesus." They live in a private spiritual world. They would never think of having this kind of relationship with anyone. This is an impoverished existence.

Voluntarily open your heart to the insight of a few close friends. Seek correction and reproof lest you be deceived by sin. Ask your close Christian friends to point out to you what they think is the major area in which you need to grow.

I have personally experienced the love of friends in Christ keeping me sensitive to sin and Gospel holiness. One of them called one day just to encourage me. When they heard the tone in my voice, they could tell I was falling into a bad habit of overwork. I was neglecting my family. They threatened to come for a visit and snap me in line, with my wife's assistance. I told them I would slow down. They asked, "When?" I told them I would have more time in ten more days and then I would take a break. They would not let me off the hook. They challenged me to trust God with my work, come home, and pay attention to my family. I went home early that day and did so. I was so grateful for someone who watched for my soul.

If this were common in the body of Christ, how many infections of sin would be nipped in the bud? We need to cultivate in our churches the expectation that people have a few spiritual friends, who keep an eye on them and vice versa! Then we need to coach them in how wisely to address a concern when they feel a drifting in someone's heart and a change in their behavior.

Let's look at a few more principles. First, it should be evident we are dealing with sin, not violation of church taboos or traditions. We must be careful not to go to a brother or sister for "sin" for which I have no biblical basis. This takes great care.

Consider the religious people of Israel in Jesus' day. They had developed a use of the law as a hedge against evil. Taking the commandments of God, they had developed an extensive list of applications. They were comprehensive. People no longer had to think about their walk with God. They simply followed the details of the code book. Jesus came and violated some of their rules. He rebuked them for elevating their traditions to the status of Scripture.

There is no sin in moderate use of alcohol. There is no sin in being overweight (it may be a thyroid condition). There is no sin in driving a fire-engine-red car. However, I have known well-meaning believers who admonished others for all of these. I have no authority to stand in the place of God and come up with my own list of sin.

Make sure that the sin you are seeing in the other can be addressed by reading a verse of Scripture, without commentary. For example, perhaps you think a sister you know is becoming greedy. The proof of this is her purchase of a nice car. So, what verse reproves her? Is it 1 John 2:15 "Love not the world"? Will she see the application without any comment from you? Even if you make the connection of this to her car, are you certain of her motive?

Contrast that with a brother who is often belittling others in the church. How far do you need to go to address this? There are multiple verses on gossip and slander. Read these and you may make your point with minimal or no comment.

What about concerns for motives? Perhaps that woman is becoming worldly. Then address it as a concern. Ask her to search her own heart, but only after there is considerable reason for the suspicion.

Second, I must guard the church against an atmosphere that is always pointing out sin. I think Scripture speaks to this on two fronts. It addresses the danger of a judgmental spirit, and it speaks of love's making kind judgments of others. For example:

udge not, that you be not judged. For with
the judgment you pronounce you will be
judged, and with the measure you use it will
be measured to you. Why do you see the speck
that is in your brother's eye, but do not notice
the log that is in your own eye? Or how can
you say to your brother, "Let me take the
speck out of your eye," when there is the log
in your own eye? You hypocrite, first take the
log out of your own eye, and then you will
see clearly to take the speck out of your
brother's eye. (Matt. 7:1–5).

The issue at hand is not whether we should ever
judge others, but how we should do so. Our faults
are far less apparent to us than the faults of others.
Jesus is saying, first focus on your own life. When
you see yourself clearly, you will be more able to
help another.

The people who are most severe in judgment of
others are usually people who are very blind to
themselves. They think they are righteous. Their
tendency to see faults in others and none in
themselves is a form of self-righteousness.

Take this passage as an example of charitable
judgment: "Hatred stirs up strife, but love covers
all offenses" (Prov. 10:12). It means there is a place
for patience, for assuming the best of motives unless
there is sufficient cause to hold this in question.

One could only imagine a local church where
there was constant correction of each other. There
would be no time for anything else. There would
be no place for forbearance. The atmosphere would

be poisonous. The call to reprove my fellow believer for sin must be put in the context of the call to encourage them and build them up.

Our merciful God does not number our sins. If he did, none could stand (Ps. 130:2). Jesus did not rebuke the disciples for every offense. There is a proper place for love that covers a multitude of sins. People need room to grow and an atmosphere that permits this.

Third, the general tone of the New Testament is encouragement. This does not mean there is no place for reproof. We build character and godliness by listening to reproof. However, we wear people down by constant reproof.

The assumption of Jesus' words is that the sin was observable. "If your brother sins" means it is a sin which you have seen. There is no call in Matthew for an atmosphere of suspicion. There is a call to deal with the obvious. In our age of psychological reading between the lines, we must be careful.

Paul spells out the goal of ministry. "The goal of this command is love, which comes from a pure heart and a good conscience and a sincere faith" (1 Tim. 1:5) These are buoyant qualities.

I have sat under ministries that always left me feeling weighted and discouraged. There was a constant reminder of sin, a constant call to introspective judgment. At first, I considered this a mark of a high view of holiness. Then as I read the epistles, I noted that the tone of the Apostles is one of hope and encouragement and joy. Believers are called to remember the sin they have been rescued from, but the call to holiness is more focused on the confidence we have in the Spirit to grow.

Here is what makes Christianity different than religion. The Jews of Jesus' day were religious. They had no tolerance for sinners. People who sinned were discouraged and without hope. They were shocked that Jesus welcomed them. They concluded he must be soft on sin. Jesus made clear that he was more holy than they. At the same time he was more willing to embrace people in their flawed condition than the Pharisees.

I find it helpful to assume that another believer wants to please God. Therefore they welcome my encouragement. The attitude behind reproof is to help them grow in Christ, which they want to do. Whereas if I assume they are disinterested, or hostile, I will approach them with harshness.

Fourth, there is the sin that is the normal lapse of the believer in their state of remaining corruption. The first question to ask is simple: *Is this sin I am seeing part of the ordinary stumbling of the Christian?* If so, then I need not speak to it immediately. Is it hardening their hearts or are they judging it themselves? If the latter, I may forbear.

This does not mean those faults are any less sin. It may deeply grieve their conscience before God. Nevertheless, it may be the normal lapse. First John does say he wrote that we might not sin. He does not say, that we "might not sin much." However, the context (1:5–2:2) is one of encouragement that when we do sin and admit it we have an advocate with the Father. Denying we have sinned is a mark of darkness. Being discouraged by sin is a mark of denial of the cross. Sometimes our ministry is one of encouragement.

Years ago I was loathing myself for the sins that I repeated habitually. I was a new Christian and had brought some dirty laundry with me into the kingdom. A godly man reminded me that the Lord had pity on me, as a father does his children (Ps. 103:13–14). That truth has helped me when I stumble and given me gentleness in dealing with others.

Fifth, we must take into account the work of the Spirit. He is wisely shaping us into the likeness of Christ in his sovereign love. Rather than expose all our corruption at once, he is gentle. To see ourselves as God sees us would undo us. He points out one thing at a time. As I intend to reprove someone or speak to them of my concern for them in sin, I must be aware of this.

One of the most amazing examples of this came from a friend in ministry. In the previous year, a man had come to faith out of a foul-mouthed and licentious life. There was great change of heart and behavior, but there were times he slipped and uttered a curse word while talking to folks at church. This was embarrassing to all. What was to be done?

The pastor weighed out an appropriate response. If he focused on just this sin, he would be narrow in focus, for he knew the man battled with may other lusts. He decided to be patient and to pray.

For What Sins?

A few weeks later, the man approached him and told him he needed to talk. Finding a private setting, the pastor heard the man spill his heart. However, he was surprised. In essence, here is what the man said,

> Pastor, I can't believe how much God is at work in me. You know how I love my motorboats? I polish it every week and try to find some time to go out on the lake every weekend. I sometimes neglect my family when I do that. Well, God has told me that it is an idol and I need to get rid of it. I need help. I don't know what I will do without it but I want to trust God and obey.

My friend said he would not have guessed this sin in ten years! He was amazed at how the Holy Spirit worked. Therefore, he counseled the man to put an ad in the paper and sell it. He went home to do that. The next day, he returned almost beside himself with joy. When he arrived at his house, he began to clean the boat and make it ready for sale. A car passed by and stopped. The driver exited and walked up to him. Then he inquired about whether the boat was for sale! When the stunned new Christian asked him to name a price he would pay, the man named the exact amount he had planned to ask for in his advertisement. He sold it on the spot.

Here the pastor saw that his role was to encourage and to pray. God did the work. He might also have come alongside the man and asked him how he could pray for him.

Sixth, where the believer is judging his sin and admitting it, I have no reason to be harsh. They, like me, are seeking help and encouragement to keep on fighting the holy war. It is not helpful to rub salt in a wound.

More than once I have counseled a man or woman who comes with tears, broken over the power of sin in their lives. This is especially true with sexual sins of any form. I must be careful not to break the bruised reed of their souls with undue harshness. There must be a self-judgment of the sin. If there is, we can help the person grow.

Seventh, sometimes we must intervene quickly. Look at Paul's concern in 1 Corinthians 5 with public sin. Some transgressions are private. Others are public. The list given seems to deal with a believer who has a reputation for these things. Moreover, the sins are evident to others. Immorality, adultery, greed that is evident, idolatry, or swindling and slandering – these are often public offenses.

Some sins also have an unusual seriousness to them. If I see a friend flirting with someone of the opposite sex, it is not time to be patient. It is time, with wise and gracious words, to intervene, see if are suspicions are correct, and seek their repentance before adultery is committed.

All these principles provide a tempering against a campaign of excessive moral zeal. If the church is only for people who have their moral act together, at least on the outside, then how are we different than the religious elites of Jesus' day? How is this good news to the broken and stained mass of humanity?

No, we function as followers of Jesus pursuing Gospel holiness. We seek the humility to face our own sin and confess it to others. We invite them into our lives for correction. In addition, we are so bound to each other that we watch out for any offenses in each others lives that need reproof. Most of all, we encourage each other in this hard battle against sin. In addition, at times, reprove each other because of our love for Christ.

5

Go to Your Brother Alone

The point is that sin has to be dealt with. It isn't enough to make announcements or to post rules. It isn't enough just to give commands. . .there has to be an enforcement of those.

John MacArthur

*****

I know men who have fought in wars. They stood against powerful enemies. They battled tanks and powerful weapons. Against incredible odds and with great sacrifice they stood their ground. They are men of courage. Yet they tremble in the presence of a confrontation. They run from looking someone in the eye and speaking to them in a way that is personal, and emotionally charged. Jesus said, "Go to your brother alone." They reply, "I'll just let it pass. It's not a big deal."

I know many who have misjudged others. They saw something happen and they interpreted it. They told others their mis-judgment as though it was a fact. Jesus said, "Go to your brother alone."

I have listened to holy gossip. This is usually negative information shared about others with the intent of soliciting prayer, "Pray for Bill and Mary. I hear they are thinking of a divorce." Jesus said, "Go to your brother alone."

Jesus' words are clear. When I have a concern for a brother or sister, when their behavior leaves me with doubts about their future holiness, when I see them doing something wrong, I am to go to them alone. We are to speak to a brother or sister. We are not to talk about them. Jesus said, "Go to your brother alone."

But why? Why should we go alone, speak to them in private? What could be wrong with telling a few others, getting advice along the way? Let's not be too fussy. Let me enjoy a little inside trading on bad news. Why should I go alone? As always, there is wisdom and righteousness behind the command of God.

Most Christians understand that the Name and honor of God are to be protected. We pray, "Let your name be hallowed." Our living should enhance God's reputation. That is what it means to glorify him.

We often do not realize that God is jealous for our reputation. We bear his image. We are made in his likeness. We are crowned with dignity and honor. God has placed us in societies. In every culture, people evaluate and judge others based upon their experience of their behavior. This is our reputation. A good name is more desired than riches. God has specifically given commands that call us to protect the name of another. Here are specific texts which speak to this:

> A good name is more desirable than great riches; to be esteemed is better than silver or gold. (Prov. 22:1).

> A good name is better than fine perfume. (Eccles. 7:1).

> And we are sending along with him the brother who is praised by all the churches for his service to the gospel. What is more, he was chosen by the churches to accompany us as we carry the offering, which we administer in order to honor the Lord himself and to show our eagerness to help. We want to avoid any criticism of the way we administer this liberal gift. For we are taking pains to do what is right, not only in the eyes of the Lord but also in the eyes of men. In addition, we are sending with them our brother who has often proved to us in many ways that he is zealous, and now even more so because of his great confidence in you. (2 Cor. 8:18–22).

Here are a series of passages which complement each other. Paul is describing a man, anonymously, who enjoys the fragrance of a good reputation. He is so respected that Paul and the churches choose him to be one of the bearers of the large mercy-gift to be taken to the impoverished Jerusalem church. This man is praised by all the churches.

Paul further indicates that there is nothing wrong with this plan. He is not being political. He is being wise. He says, in essence, that reputation is valuable. Choosing a man so esteemed to assist in a mission that could go awry by mismanagement or misappropriation of funds is godly. He says he took pains to do what was right in the eyes of men. The man's reputation for zeal is deserved.

Reputation is a good thing. Consider the qualifications of leaders. When the Twelve look for help in a potentially divisive situation, they say "Brothers, choose seven men from among you who are known to be full of the Spirit and wisdom."(Acts 6:4) They had a reputation which preceded them.

The same is true when Paul arrived in Lystra. Timothy had a reputation. "He came to Derbe and then to Lystra, where a disciple named Timothy lived...The brothers at Lystra and Iconium spoke well of him"(Acts 16:1–2). The outcome is Paul's choice of Timothy to accompany him on his journeys.

Later Paul instructs Timothy to make sure that his deacons are men known and respected by all.

> He must also have a good reputation with outsiders, so that he will not fall into disgrace and into the devil's trap. Deacons, likewise, are to be men worthy of respect, sincere, not indulging in much wine, and not pursuing dishonest gain. . . . They must first be tested; and then if there is nothing against them, let them serve as deacons. (1 Tim. 3:7–10).

Go to Your Brother Alone

In addition, John speaks of a faithful servant of Christ named Demetrius, who has received a good testimony from everyone, and from the truth itself (3 John 12). We need go no further with this. Reputation is God's idea.

God's concern for reputation is also seen in a mass of commands regarding slander and gossip. This begins with "Do not bear false witness against your neighbor." The sin involved is both a sin against the truth and a sin against another's honor. The Old and New Testament elaborate on many occasions.

> Do not go about spreading slander among your people. (Lev. 19:16).

There are two sins against reputation: gossip and slander. Gossip is spreading information to people who have neither responsibility nor authority to do anything about it. It may be true, but it is not to be shared. Slander is spreading a lie about someone else.

I have seen good men ruined by careless gossip or malicious slander. Churches have been divided. Marriages have ended. Careers come to a tragic end. Income is lost. Friends are left in confusion.

God loves truth and that includes the truth about others. God hates slander and even establishes punishments for it in cases of criminal accusation.

> If a malicious witness takes the stand to accuse a man of a crime, the two men involved in the dispute must stand in the presence of the

> LORD before the priests and the judges who are in office at the time. The judges must make a thorough investigation, and if the witness proves to be a liar, giving false testimony against his brother, then do to him as he intended to do to his brother. You must purge the evil from among you. (Deut. 19:16–19).

False witnesses are to meet with the punishment that would have fallen to the object of their malice. This is appropriate because most often slander and gossip are a form of revenge. Pettiness and cowardice combine with malice to use words as daggers.

There are many other sins against reputation. Commenting on the nineth comm-andment, the Westminster Catechism puts it this way:

> Question 144
> What are the duties required in the ninth commandment?

> Answer
> The duties required in the ninth commandment are, *the preserving and promoting of truth between man and man and the good name of our neighbor, as well as our own* ; appearing and standing for the truth; and from the heart, sincerely, freely, clearly, and fully, *speaking the truth, and only the truth* in matters of judgment and justice, and in all other things whatsoever . . . a ready receiving of a good report and *unwillingness to admit of an evil report. . . discouraging talebearers*, flatterers, and slanderers. . .

Question 145
What are the sins forbidden in the ninth commandment?

Answer
The sins forbidden in the ninth commandment are . . . *speaking untruth, lying, slandering, backbiting, detracting, tale bearing, whispering, scoffing, reviling, rash, harsh, and partial censuring; mis-constructing intentions, words, and actions* . . . unnecessary discovering of infirmities; raising false rumors, receiving and countenancing evil reports; evil suspicion (my italics)

In essence, God loves the truth. He loves the truth about himself and the truth about you. The highlighted portions give every reason from the mind of God for why Jesus said I must go alone.

We must not forget the commands of God are expressions of love for God and love for my brother. Love would lead me in the path Jesus prescribes.

My obligation is to love my brother. If he has sinned love owes him the opportunity to repent without embarrassment. If I have misunderstood, love owes him the opportunity to clear my misperceptions. This is central.

We are not talking about law breaking but love breaking. An older couple, when admonished to stop gossiping, retort, "We can tell anyone we please." Their words reveal a heart without love for the brother and sister they slander.

Going alone means being direct. Sometimes people will do anything to avoid being direct. The consequences are often twisted. I have a good friend who pastored a church for over a decade. He was loved and esteemed by many of the people. He and his wife raised their children in the church. With the passing of time, however, a number of the leaders of the church believed he was a hindrance to their growth. They concluded that he needed to move on.

However, their plan of attack was not one of truthtelling. It was a plan for conversations among themselves, creating suspicion, and trying to "improve" him. No one sat down and said, "I am concerned for your ability to lead us. I would like to discuss this. My goal is not to hurt you in any way but to find what is best for you and us." Instead, they hinted and pressured. He did not take their hints.

In such an atmosphere, every foible becomes exaggerated. This was no exception. This pastor became the object of a rumor, a rumor that he was pursuing a woman in the church.

Finally, it was decided to bring in a consultant. His mission was to take a survey of the leaders. Everyone participated in developing the survey except the pastor. It included a question pertaining to the confidence of people in his ability to take them into their future. When the survey results came in, it was the consultant that broke the news to him. His reputation was not valued. They did not love the truth. They shunned directness. This happens all the time in churches. It is called politics. People who play politics are cowards.

We are to hate slander and gossip. Because it is

so common, it is very difficult to maintain a zero-tolerance for slander. Amy Carmichael held the highest standards for unity and love in the Dohnavur Fellowship in India. Her rule of love was simple: the absent are always safe with us. She disciplined and even removed people from her team of workers when they violated this rule! Calvary's love compelled her.

What do we do when we live amidst a gossiping community? For many years I have kept the words of Charles Simeon in my journal. Simeon pastored in Cambridge for over fifty years. His influence was profound, but he lived with a slanderous congregation and community. He developed a caution about such matters, having felt the sting of them many times.

> The longer I live the more I feel the importance of adhering to the rules which I have laid down for myself in such matters. First, to hear as little as possible what is to the prejudice of others. Second, to believe nothing of the kind until I am absolutely forced to. Third, never drink into the spirit of one who circulates an ill report. Fourth, always to believe that if the other side were heard, a very different account would be given of the matter. I consider love as wealth; and as I would resist a man who should come to rob my house, so would I a man who would weaken my regard for any human being.[1]

1. Cited in a lecture on Charles Simeon, personal notes of Mark Lauterbach

Simeon understood that this is a matter of love and truth. It is a protection of reputation.

Not only is such one-to-one confrontation necessary for the sake of truth and the reputation of my brother, but also for the sake of relationship. What happens when I, in love, go to a brother or sister, and speak to them about a concern they may have? What I fear is that they will reject me, become angry and defensive, or lie. What may happen, and often does happen, is quite the opposite. They become a closer friend than we have known before. In addition, they know they are loved.

We have friends who worked in campus ministry for many years. They gave themselves body and soul to the students. Their home was constantly full of collegians. Their evenings were booked with discipleship and entertainment. They served in their local church as well. They worked hard.

They also began to neglect each other. Their marriage was stagnant at best. Remoteness set in. All this was apparently private, but the signs of erosion began to show. Some student leaders noticed. They were married and they understood marriage. They also could see the warning signs. They wondered what to do. It was frightening to consider going to them. Nevertheless, they knew it was right to do so. After much prayer, they set up a time and waded in. I only heard about this later from both couples.

Yes, they said, it was awkward. It is hard for a twenty year old to raise very personal issues with people fifteen years their senior. They knew that a broken marriage would dishonor Christ and a poor marriage would hinder their usefulness. With fear and trembling they raised their concerns. The ministry couple was overwhelmed. Someone noticed! They were embarrassed. Moreover, they were also shocked that they were loved. They wept for such love. They faced their sin and repented. It became a turning point for their marriage and their ministry.

In addition, the two couples became endeared to each other. A bond was formed that has lasted for years. As the story was told, many were encouraged to follow God's path.

So, how is this to be done? First, ask yourself this simple question: *Knowing what I know, if I loved this brother or sister as Christ, what would I do to pursue their eternal good?* Jesus said that true love calls me to lay down my life for a brother. Love calls me to action. Paul defended his rebuke of the Corinthians by asserting his love. Only false friends restrain themselves from reproof.

> Better is open rebuke than hidden love.
> Faithful are the wounds of a friend; profuse
> are the kisses of an enemy (Prov. 27:5–6).

Second, you must fight fear. Fear is a great hindrance. (Lovelessness is the first). I have been too afraid to speak humbly to a brother or sister about their walk with Jesus. Sometimes my failure seemed to result in their stumbling further into sin.

I once thought that fear was a worry over how they would respond. No one enjoys a nasty confrontation. I once thought it was due to a concern with their feelings. I did not want to hurt them. I now believe it is a form of protecting me from the turmoil and the possible rejection. Ultimately my fear is rooted in excessive love of my self and my comfort.

If I see how God sees at all I will know that sin is destructive, that admonition must take place. Again, let me allow Bonhoeffer to speak:

> Reproof is unavoidable. God's Word demands it when a brother falls into open sin. The practice of discipline in the congregation begins in the smallest circles. Where defection from God's Word in doctrine or life imperils the family fellowship and with it the whole congregation, the word of admonition and rebuke must be ventured (Life Together[1], 107).

Have I persuaded you? We are to love each other fervently as brothers and sisters. This means there is a proper covering over of the sins of each other, but there is also proper exposure and correction where the dangers loom large.

Third, you must clothe yourself with the greatest humility. Paul puts it this way:

> Brothers, if anyone is caught in any transgression, you who are spiritual should

---

1. *Life Together*, Dietrich Bonheoffer, Harper and Row, New York, 1954

restore him in a spirit of gentleness. Keep watch
on yourself, lest you too be tempted (Gal. 6:1).

Admonition from the vantage point of arrogance
is ugly and unhelpful. My ability to discover
"specks" and be blind to my own "beams" should
guard my heart. Dietrich Bonhoeffer speaks to this
with a fresh insight:

> The basis upon which Christians can speak
> to one another is that each knows the other
> as a sinner, who, with all his human dignity,
> is lonely and lost if he is not given help. This
> recognition gives to our brotherly speech the
> freedom and candor that it needs. We speak
> to one another on the basis of the help we
> both need. We admonish one another to go
> the way that Christ bids us to go. We warn
> one another against the disobedience that is
> our common destruction. We are gentle and
> we are severe with one another, for we know
> both God's kindness and God's severity. Why
> should we be afraid of one another, since both
> of us have only God to fear? Why should we
> think that our brother would not understand
> us, when we understood very well what was
> meant when somebody spoke God's comfort
> or God's admonition to us, perhaps in words
> that were halting and unskilled? Or do we
> really think there is a single person in this
> world that does not need either
> encouragement or admonition? Why, then,
> has God bestowed Christian brotherhood
> upon us? *(Life Together, pp 105–6)*.

Now that we have the right motives, how is all this to be approached? Proverbs is filled with guidelines of wisdom. God made us a certain way and we are to live with the order of his creation. Choose your words carefully. Recognize that people are fragile. Gentleness is required. Exposing sin can be shattering to someone unless done with a kind word. Soft words can break the bone. Grievous words stir up anger.

I once worked for a man who was blunt. No, he was beyond blunt. I went through a stage of hating him. This was a problem. He was a brother! I wanted to slander him. I wanted to avoid him. I finally got up the courage and went to see him. I did not speak out of love, but I spoke clearly. He responded humbly. Through following Matthew 18 we became the best of friends. It was through this I learned to be gentle and encouraged him to be the same.

Next, make time to be with the person in an unrushed environment but do it quickly after you tell them you want to meet with them. There is nothing worse than waiting two weeks after a brother tells me he has something personal to talk with you about! Carve out the time. Fear makes us want to do "hit and run" admonition. Fear makes us want to write a note, an e-mail, or make a phone call. Face to face is the preferred method. Eye contact and body language are powerful tools.

Then, assume you have misunderstood. State it that way. Most of the time, we have misread the situation. You are there to get the facts, not hold an inquisition. I have even said, "This just can't be true but I want to clear up my misunderstanding."

Fourth, give them time to talk. You have just taken their psychological clothes off. They are fragile. You are not there to accuse but to clarify. If there is sin, you are there to call them to freedom from sin. They will need to respond.

Fifth, be ready for a variety of responses. They can get angry, defensive, quiet, submissive, and later avoid you like the plague. Do not judge them too quickly though. Few enjoy reproof. Much of the time they will become better friends! However, be ready to be deceived too.

I received a phone call one afternoon from a man in our church. He was in anguish. His wife was packing to leave him and go back home. Their marriage had been troubled at best. We had done some pastoral counseling. Now it looked like it was over.

I went to their house with another staff member. As Mary explained her reasons, all the while packing, I asked her where she planned to meet Dave once she was out of the city. She stopped dead in her tracks. She wondered how I knew.

Dave was a leader in the church. He and his wife had been part of the counseling help for this couple. They had befriended them. Nevertheless, it seemed to have gone beyond friendship. One month before, I had met Dave for breakfast. Over the previous months I had observed his spending a large amount of time with Mary. She had been fairly affectionate with him in the presence of his own wife! I asked him to assure me there was a misunderstanding. He did. He said their relationship was platonic and ministry-based. He had lied.

It was obvious to me what was going on in Mary's heart. As soon as I revealed the sin, she broke, changed her heart, asked her husband to stay with her, and called Dave and told him it was off. Dave came to me and said it was all true. He had been saving money for this trip and had a letter to be mailed to his wife asking for a divorce. He refused to repent. The situation became very ugly.

As I reflected back on that sad situation I was glad that I had gone to him earlier, as soon as I had concerns. I spoke with him in private, just between the two of us. I had done my part in winning him. I could do nothing about his lying to me. However, I had loved him as a brother.

This is what Jesus calls us to. The response is not our worry. Loving each other enough to clarify and admonish is.

> Nothing can be crueler than the tenderness that consigns another to his sin. Nothing can be more compassionate than the severe rebuke that calls a brother back from the path of sin (*Life Together*, p.107).

6

The Church and Israel

Discipline hath been metamorphosed into a hideous monster, an engine of...domination and tyranny, for . . .the terror of the souls of men, and the destruction of their lives with all their earthly concern, unto the erection of a tyrannical empire

John Owen

*****

When churches take the processes of Matthew 18 seriously for the first time, they are apt to go to extremes. The process becomes rigid and harsh. It is wooden and leaves no room for patience. Matthew did not intend for such a pattern to take place.

Sometimes zealous practitioners become busybodies and fail to honor the Holy Spirit as he works in the lives of their fellow-believers. They allow no time for his work and proceed to admonish each other for every sin. They apply the principles woodenly and with severity, creating an environment for folks of Olympic-quality self-discipline.

The church is not a community of elite troops, filtered and sifted until only the most pure emerge. Moving with the movers is not the nature of local church ministry. The Apostles do not dismiss the saints who struggle with sin. They encourage them to follow Christ, with humility and truthfulness.

I remember my first experience with church discipline. Tom and Helen were co-workers in ministry. They met serving Christ together. Their love and friendship was apparent to all. Their peers respected them. I was asked to perform their wedding. My time with them in pre-marital counseling was not complicated. They both came into the marriage free from previous immorality. They both had good families. They both appeared to be growing in Christ.

I was stunned when they began to have problems. Tom came with a list of difficulties he had with Helen. She did not smile when they played tennis. She did not vacuum the rug in parallel lines. She did not cook food the way he wanted.

These problems were faced head on. We spoke to realistic expectations, respect for individuality, and his calling to love her. She was not his slave! I thought we were making progress after a few months. However, Tom had just told me he was going to divorce his wife. After less than two years of marriage, he believed their differences were beyond reconciliation. He wanted a wife he could shape as he pleased. His list of ways she could improve was three pages long. She absolutely refused to pursue divorce. She resisted the plan he developed to end their marriage. This was my first confrontation with flagrant sin.

I reflected on my commitment to Matthew 18 as a process of discipline. It seemed clear enough. I went to him alone. He refused. A week later, I took a pastor friend with me. The stubborn resistance continued. I spoke to the Board and recommended a letter be sent, after review by legal counsel.

The Board balked. They were concerned about the hastiness of the action. They wondered whether Matthew 18 really applied. After some deliberation, they agreed to send their own team to see Jim. They came back at the next meeting recommending his removal from the church. We excommunicated him and reported this to the next business meeting of the church. Simple enough, we thought.

So it seemed. While I believe the process is simple, I reflect back on this my first course of action in discipline and believe I made the error of treating this one passage as though it was the whole of Scripture. Why did I not take more time to pursue him? Why did I not engage more of his friends in seeking to win him? Why did I not weep more for his sin? My approach was stiff and bureaucratic. Follow steps one, two, and three – and be done with it. I do not know if the result would have been any better, but I could have been more patient.

I came to ask these questions: Is Matthew 18 a one-two-three process? Is it to take place in three weeks? Does it have some flexibility and patience to it? If the goal is winning our brother, should we not be forbearing as God is forbearing with us? What is the nature of this process?

Those questions are answered by recognizing that Jesus is transferring authority from Israel to the church. The pattern of Matthew 18 is rooted in Old Testament judicial procedures.

Israel was given authority to execute justice among its people. They were a nation. They were a holy people, to live under Yahweh's word and rule. His peculiar people had civic functions as well as religious ones. They did this to represent the kingdom of God on earth.

There would be sin in Israel. It must be addressed. Very specific stipulations were given to guarantee a careful procedure. Specific sanctions were imposed depending on the nature of the crime. They needed to make sure they followed justice. Justice is a treasured practice in the Mosaic Law:

> You shall appoint judges and officers in all your towns that the LORD your God is giving you, according to your tribes, and they shall judge the people with righteous judgment. Do not pervert justice or show partiality. Do not accept a bribe, for a bribe blinds the eyes of the wise and twists the words of the righteous. Follow justice and justice alone, so that you may live and possess the land the LORD your God is giving you. (Deut. 16:18–20).

Humans of character were to be given the authority to judge. They had to be people who loved truth and justice even in the face of bribery or the temptation of favoritism.

These judges were to be distributed throughout the communities of Israel so that it was not difficult to have access to them. God speaks against all forms of distorting justice. They were to take special care that the poor and powerless not be oppressed.

As Israel developed as a nation, they discarded these commands. Their failure to protect the helpless brought God's judgment. Their favor to the rich and powerful at the expense of truth cost them dearly. A quick read through the prophets reveals God's hatred for their sin and a call to repentance.

> Wash yourselves; make yourselves clean; remove the evil of your deeds from before my eyes; cease to do evil, learn to do good; seek justice, correct oppression; bring justice to the fatherless, plead the widow's cause
> (Is. 1:16–17).

It is not easy to practice truthfulness and to measure all by the same standard. The rule of law, which we value in certain parts of the world, pictures justice as blind to the persons, measuring all charges in the objective scales of principle. This is rooted in the Old Testament where the pattern for investigation and execution are spelled out clearly:

> If there is found among you, within any of your towns that the LORD your God is giving you, a man or woman who does what is evil in the sight of the LORD your God, in transgressing his covenant, and has gone and served other gods and worshiped them, or the sun or the moon or any of the host of heaven, which I have forbidden, and it is told you and you hear of it, then you shall inquire diligently, and if it is true and certain that such an abomination has been done in Israel, then you shall bring out to your gates that man or woman who has done this evil thing, and you shall stone that man or woman to death with stones. On the evidence of two witnesses or of three witnesses the one who is to die shall be put to death; a person shall not be put to death on the evidence of one witness. The hand of the witnesses shall be first against him to put him to death, and afterward the hand of all the people. So you shall purge the evil from your midst (Deut. 17:2–7).

Here there is allegation of idolatry. The first assumption is that the person is innocent until proven guilty. Because this was the case, this allegation is to be pursued with diligent inquiry. Rumors and hearsay must not be acted upon. Only when it is established as true and certain may action be taken. I think it is from a passage like this that the idea of "due diligence" arose – doing everything humanly possible to get at the facts.

It is the reason that all sides must be heard. I have never engaged in this kind of investigation where I heard the same story from the major parties involved. We all slant the truth, give our perspective. We filter what we want to hear and see in order to prove our point.

This is why one witness is not enough to convict a man accused of any crime or offense he may have committed. A matter must be established by the testimony of two or three witnesses. This was not an absolute guarantee as trials could be rigged, such as the trial of Jesus.

Love for truth and justice must rule. This is an objective proceeding. Emotion is to be taken out of the equation. Even when the offender is a family member, or there are accompanying signs or wonders, the execution is to take place (see Deuteronomy 13). The witnesses must be the first to begin the execution.

Let's clarify further. Sin was and is an issue among the people of God. The Law of Moses taught the people that sin was a very real concern to a holy God, who lived among his people. In order to have such a God among them, they had sacrifices to offer when they discovered they had sinned. What is not always understood is that such sacrifices were only for sins committed unknowingly.

However, what do we mean by sin? It is any transgression of the law of God. What if they did not know the law? God taught his people that sin is sin even when they did not know it was sin.

If a person sins and does what is forbidden in any of the Lord's commands, even though he does not know it, he is guilty and will be held responsible (Lev. 5:17).

For those with modern sensibilities, this seems strange. Nevertheless, God wanted it to be clear that the guilt of sin rested on an objective standard, and ignorance was not an excuse. This may seem severe but we must remember that all sin was worthy of capital punishment in the Garden of Eden and it was only the mercy of God that did not punish all this way.

The second principle is simple: sin must be atoned for. It could not be swept under the rug. God was gracious. He did not punish all sin immediately. He provided a way by which his sinning people could maintain fellowship with him. When the sin was realized, the Israelite brought a sacrifice, made confession over it, and it was slain in their place. This was true for individuals, leaders, or even the nation as a whole. It was a constant reminder of the proper judgment of sin and the mercy of God in providing a substitute.

Here is the surprise. The laws of Leviticus made no provision for sins committed with premeditated planning. It was here that the laws of civil punishment seemed to apply and various penalties were exacted. The lesson is clear: sin is serious and it corrupts the people of God.

Third, God entrusted the process of facing sin head on to sinners! This is a great difficulty. Humanity, being what it is, easily falls prey to slanderous accusation, distorted facts, defensiveness, headstrong actions, and biased conclusions. Therefore, God gave explicit guidelines for the administration of justice and the judgment of sin among his people. Here God speaks to all of these potential distortions, and processes are established to protect the innocent and determine where and if there is guilt.

The justice of the Old Covenant assumes we are innocent until proven guilty. For example, when a house owner assaults a thief in the dark, the person who kills them is not guilty. They could not see what they were doing! There is no way to determine whether they intended to kill or were just acting in self-defense (Exod. 22:3).

The same is true when a man is charged with raping a betrothed woman. If it takes place in the country, she is presumed innocent for she may have cried out and not been heard (Deut. 22:25–27). If it was in the city and she did not cry out, she is a willing partner for no one heard her cry.

How does this relate to Matthew 18? According to 1 Peter 2:9, the church is now the "elect race, the royal priesthood, the holy nation." We are the new people of God on earth. His kingdom is now the church. The reality of sin will still be present among the new people of God.

So how does she pursue justice? How does she deal with sin since she has no power of capital punishment? As we have seen, the church is not a political entity. If that is so, what powers does she have to uphold the rule of God in her midst? This is the question Matthew 18 addresses, and it is built upon the foundation of all the Mosaic legislation on justice.

The fundamental guiding passage is the one Jesus cites in Matthew 18: the urgency of making sure the facts of the case are clear and there is eyewitness testimony by more than one person. This is addressed in Deuteronomy 17:6 and 19:15.

> One witness is not enough to convict a man accused of any crime or offense he may have committed. A matter must be established by the testimony of two or three witnesses.

The passage is quite limiting. There is even provision for judgment of the malicious witness.

The point is this: the pursuit of sufficient testimony is not a "step" in the process but a hedge against headstrong or wrongful punishment. Our own sin can make us cowards and it also makes us hasty and harsh. Jesus is not giving a simple "go with two others" as something to do. In that phrase is the notion of "do a careful investigation; make sure you have the facts." It is a protection against slander and rumor.

Who has not seen the power of rumor, hearsay, gossip, and slander in the church? A rumor began that wounded the heart of a deacon, that he was seen kissing a young woman in the back of the church. It had spread from person to person in an air of holy concern before someone finally spoke to him. The facts were that he had kissed his daughter goodbye after escorting her to the back of the parking lot after a prayer meeting. Since the person who saw this did not know his daughter, they jumped to conclusions.

One of the most difficult situations I have known was resolved in my heart with these principles. A troubled adult woman, in counseling, was convinced she had recovered memories of abuse in her childhood. Another member of the family was the guilty party. She, with her counselor, came to ask me to "deal with the offending party." They went beyond that; the woman personally accused him of the crime. When he denied the actions, they insisted he was "in denial." I was expected, based upon her vague recovered memories, to begin a disciplinary process.

This was very difficult. Here were conflicting testimonies. Here was a counselor who assured me this woman was telling me the truth and I was furthering her victimization by not dealing with the accused in discipline. I was also told that I needed to speak to her father as he was guilty of neglect. In addition, the father told me he would hold me accountable for how this was handled. About this time I was ready to change occupations.

I meditated and sought counsel. Based on the passages cited above, I refused to take action. Moses insisted on clarity. There were not two or three witnesses! I could do nothing except take sides. The woman was enraged and left the church. The accused pieced his life back together. The family was never the same because of the slanderous way this had been approached.

Yes, there are sins committed which have only one witness, the victim. I can envision a time when that is enough, such as a rape, especially when there is physical evidence. There will be many times, however, when nothing can be done. It is one person's word against another. It would do great damage to pursue justice with such zeal that the innocent are judged. I have found encouragement in this word from Paul:

> The sins of some men are conspicuous, going before them to judgment, but the sins of others appear later (1 Tim. 5:24).

I have taken action hastily, and later regretted this when all the facts became known. Years later, the rest of the story was told, and I had totally misjudged the situation.

We could multiply stories. Jesus is not just laying out a series of simple steps. He is prescribing the care which must be taken in dealing with sin in a brother or sister in the church! The first step protects their reputation and gives opportunity for repentance with the least loss of face. The second seeks to make sure the facts are clear. This may take more than one visit.

My point is simple. Churches need to take their judicial role seriously. We are a holy people. Leaders need to be men of such character that they will wade into the tough work of ferreting out the facts and reaching conclusions. Cases of conflict may come as well. I would highly recommend the people at PeaceMaker Ministries for more resources in how conflict and mediation should be handled in the church (www.HisPeace.org).

The process of Matthew 18 also protects churches from power-wielding pastors or Boards. Power corrupts. It is not hard to imagine church leaders who rule with a heavy hand, lording it over the flock. Power tends to turn people into dictators. Dictators live above law or make laws themselves.

One significant way they may lord it over the flock is this: *telling people to leave without due process* or its counterpart *taking arbitrary actions to resolve problems without principles governing them.* Here is what this looks like. A member has a disagreement he brings to the leaders. He follows the process of Matthew 18 and speaks to them without gossip. They dislike his idea. They think he is defying their authority. They do not stand for being challenged. They tell him he is disloyal. They call him to submit. Depending on his response, they may ask him to step down from his ministry. However, they have not proven that he has done anything wrong.

They must ask him to leave *privately* because a truly biblical process would require verification and investigation, and that would prove them false. I do not believe Matthew 18 gives leaders authority to act in an arbitrary manner. It holds them accountable as well.

Truth-seeking and truth-practicing leaders make for healthy churches. There is no tolerance of politics. There is no need for gossip. Everything is clearly stated.

Church constitutions must have clear directions for how to handle such matters. There needs to be a clear appeal process for everyone. Human leaders are flawed and their decisions must be subject to scrutiny. Members need to know it is not rebellion to call leaders to account for ungodly, power-mongering actions. They also need to know that it is ungodly to stir up a split or divisions as a response. It is best in such cases to speak to the leaders, hold them to account, and then leave such leaders to their own devices.

One more point about the church as contrasted with Israel: Jesus is also making clear that the church has as its highest power the ability to excommunicate someone from its ranks with the authority of Christ himself. We are not a nation and should not wield the sword. We are a colony of heaven, the kingdom of God in local outposts, taking sin seriously but always with justice.

I must go further, however, and note this. While in Israel the process allowed for no mercy, in the church we are seeking repentance. In Israel, Achan confessed his sin. Then he was stoned. (Josh. 7:19–20). In the church, when the person has confessed, they are welcomed and embraced. The goal is not just right procedures. The goal of the right procedures is to protect and bring to repentance.

Sin will happen in the church. It is serious. The church is called to be a redemptive community. There are no sacrifices to offer, just repentance to be sought. When it faces sin in the carefulness of seeking justice and redemption, it is acting with the authority of Christ.

When discipline is lost in the church, it is a denial of her identity as the people of God on earth. When it is practiced harshly, it is just as much a denial. When truth is cherished and practiced, Christ is glorified.

7

Full Exposure

For while God has given different gifts, the most basic training he gives is meant to come from fellow Christians in everyday encounters. Church discipline is the training of the church by the church. Trained professionals have their place, but they cannot and never were meant to be a substitute for the whole body.

John White & Ken Blue

*****

My phone was blinking. A voicemail in waiting! I expected some. The previous night we had brought a matter of church discipline before the church. After months of carefully following the processes of Matthew 18 as outlined here, we had brought a man to the church for discipline. It had been years since that had been done. I did not fully understand why but later came to see how things had been done. I could sense a bit of shock and resistance.

I returned the call to hear a series of respectful protests: "Pastor. I know you are new here. You may not know that we do not do things that way here. We decided a few years ago that we should not air our dirty laundry in that way. We have delegated all this to the Board. They handle it privately. We think it will hurt the image of the church to do this publicly."

I reflected very quickly on what I heard. Had I been a rookie I might have given some ground to this man. All of these are solid concerns. Instead I simply noted that I was under orders. Jesus said "tell it to the church." He did not say "tell it to the deacons." He deferred but did not like it.

No one should doubt that proceeding down the road of Matthew 18 is exposing and shaming. It is painful to face sin squarely and do so publicly. In some cultures of the world, Matthew's commands are avoided due to an interest in face-saving. In others, they are simply ignored.

I believe that the pattern for maintaining the integrity of the people of Christ is one of the most powerful instruments of the Holy Spirit for the transformation of saints. I believe it is essential to our being light and salt in the world. I believe it is how we show to the world that we are citizens of Jesus' kingdom.

The process Jesus gave in Matthew for the maintenance of the integrity of the community of the King is wise and good. It is not malicious. It is not slanderous. It cleanses evil and brings deep repentance. It is the process of turning up the lights to expose the sin. We do this by increasing public exposure.

We need to understand that the Bible was written in the plural. It speaks to the "us" more than it speaks to the "me." People in the Western world don't get it. Americans especially cherish individualism. The Christian life is "Jesus and me" and "I go to church."

Matthew 18 belies that approach. Jesus shows that the believer is connected to a body, a local church. When I become one with Christ, he places me in his body. I am part of a family. We are interconnected. Our private lives have public implications.

The story of the sin of Achan in the book of Joshua (chapter 7) is often used to illustrate this. In a context where the entire community was under a command of God, the disobedience of one man polluted the entire nation. Paul argues that a little leaven leavens the whole lump of dough. Tolerating sin in the church corrupts all.

When I have an infection in a part of my body, my entire body is affected. A swollen thumb, damaged by a hammer, will limit my every activity.and stomach pains can immobilize me.

That's why the process of dealing with sin in the believer proceeds further. It is not "anyone else's business." If we wrote the passage it might read like this:

> If your brother sins against you, go and show
> him his sin, just between the two of you. If he
> listens, you have won your brother. If he

refuses to listen, write him off. It's none of your business. On the other hand, encourage him to leave. Better yet, tell the Board, let them take his name off the roles.

However, Jesus takes the matter to the larger family, first in two or three, then to the whole church. We have seen one reason for the process: to make sure we have the facts. There is another: the exposure of the sin to greater public view tears off the self-deceit. We are masters of pulling the wool over our own eyes.

Sin seeks the shadows. We will defend our innocence at all costs. We love the darkness because the light exposes the dirt on our souls. We love to look good to others. It is the essence of unbelief: living for the praise of men rather than the praise of God.

We love to make excuses. "I have sinned but..." is one common form of covering our tracks. We paint our transgressions as virtues – we are trying to obey and just stumbled.

For example, a number of years ago I heard a noted statesman of our country give his defense for unethical and self-serving actions. The actions were a breach of the public trust. He resigned. As he left office he explained, "I was led into a course of action which I would not normally pursue." The blame rested somewhere or other, but not on him.

The church is made up of saints who are n0t yet perfected. The doctrine of indwelling sin in the believer requires us to cease being naïve. The Spirit indwells believers. Believers have the flesh as well. All the well-worn patterns of iniquity still run in the saint. That includes hypocrisy.

How do you and I feel when we are caught by our spouses eating the cookies she made for the dinner guests? Most likely, we are angry and defensive. Why is it we waited until they left the room before we tried to snitch a few? Sin likes to hide. To deal with sin, it must be exposed. Part of the systemic nature of sin is its deceit.

The process Jesus describes is one of gradually increasing exposure. First a friend confronts, then he brings along a few others. Eyewitnesses confirm the facts but also reinforce the confrontation: this is sin, this is real, and this is destructive. The dim lights are made brighter. The facts are laid out. The individual is called to repentance.

Proverbs 26:12, 16 says that a fool is wiser in his own eyes than seven men who can render a reason. Foolishness runs in our veins. When two or three lay bare the facts of our sin, we can still deny. Teachability is not natural to the sons of Adam. We can expect angry reaction, rationalization, even an apparent willingness to talk about the problem. However, we look for repentance.

Bonhoeffer speaks to this once again; of the slippery excuses we will devise to avoid obedience:

> The human will does not want to bow before the will of God. One becomes spiteful, callous, and unrepentant toward God. People accuse

God; they ask why God has burdened them with this sickness, this death, this failure, and this marital problem. The crucial question behind all these problems is whether or not God's Word in being accepted as God's Word. Fleeing the Word of God, one submerges himself in problems in order to evade simple obedience. *Spiritual Care*, pp.33–4

I have seen the power of hypocrisy, the drive to maintain an image over a lie. I have seen it in leaders! An older man, forty-five years into marriage, had a strong ministry in his local church. He and his wife had sustained effectiveness in evangelism and discipleship. Their reputation in the broader church was impressive. However, throughout the last twenty years they had lived two lives. Their marriage was fraught with relentless conflicts. They drifted apart. He began a series of romantic liaisons.

They sought counseling, but the counseling was an attempt at self-justification. "We may have problems, but we are getting help." Finally he left her. The church was shocked.

Sadly, no attempt had ever been made to expose their hypocrisy to others. Their duplicity thrived in the shadows of a false reputation and private sin. Their public responsibilities demanded more public action. They should have resigned their leadership roles. Instead they hid.

---

1. *Spiritual Care*, Dietrich Bonhoeffer, Augsburg Fortress, Philadelphia, PA, 1985.

Full Exposure

Jesus says that increasing exposure is the path to deal with sin. The goal is confession. Confession is a simple statement of responsibility, to see things as God sees them. Repentance is a very rare thing. We cling to our image and self-sufficiency. Until we stop, we will not repent.

Secular people understand this clearly. In the 12 Steps of Alcoholics Anonymous, there is confession – public confession. Take full responsibility for your failures. My name is Fred, I am an alcoholic. No excuses, no deception, no image building. Exposure is the first step to repentance.

I have seen alcoholics deal with each other. It is ruthless. They insist on truthfulness. If one of their group says they have a "drinking problem" they insist he call himself a drunk. If they posture themselves as being in control, they counter with a litany of the damage they have done to others in their drinking.

Pride stands between us and repenting of sin.

> The root of all sin is pride, *superbia*. Confession in the presence of a brother is the profoundest kind of humiliation. It hurts, it cuts a man down, it is a dreadful blow to pride. To stand there before a brother as a sinner is an ignominy that is almost unbearable. Because this humiliation is so hard we continually scheme to evade confessing to a brother. (Dietrich Bonhoeffer, *Life Together*, pp. 113–4)

We must be careful. Confession needs to be at the appropriate level. The scope of the confession equals the scope of the transgression. That is in the process. If confronted by one and I listen, I have obviously confessed to them. If two or three come and I hear them, I have confessed to them. If I do not listen to them and the church is told, then confession must be to the church. Some sins are public by their very nature. They must be confessed publicly. One man in a church where I served was found guilty of embezzlement. It was in all the local papers. When he came for help, we asked for his confession to the church. It was already known and his repentance needed as wide an exposure with people.

Confession of sin, without excuse, without shifting blame, is the necessary first step. It is the beginning of change. It is the trip to the doctor.

Jesus gives remarkable authority to the church. He promises that he is present where the two or three gather in his name. That would seem to apply most immediately to the two or three who go to confirm the facts and expose the sin. He bestows the binding and loosing authority on the whole church. The church acts on behalf of Jesus when it is obeying Jesus' words. There is a power in such activity that this text explains.

It is such power that I believe explains what the Holy Spirit does when the church follows Matthew 18. He steps in, he breaks hardened hearts, he brings others to repentance, he makes people weep for sin, and he delivers people over to their own lusts.

I have seen only two outcomes to the process: extremely good or extremely evil. I wish I could say I have seen many acts if repentance. Most often I have found that when the process is followed, the exposure drives the person further away. Men love the darkness, rather than the light.

A pastor's wife became hypercritical. She laid all kinds of charges at the feet of the leadership – cover-up of sin, duplicity, and harshness. She left the church in anger. We discovered she was living in adultery. We admonished her. She thought she was justified. She refused any acknowledgment of sin.

Her life drifted further and further from Christ. She flirted with renouncing her faith. She began to practice lesbian relationships. When people are exposed, their hearts will be seen. It is tragic but true.

Confession may also be pursued as a means of healing when the person needs more help than can be offered privately. Often people need to tear down their false image with others so they can get help. It is the voluntary act of the repentant seeking humility. Sin can hold its power over an individual due to hypocrisy. They are living a lie. It can be effective.

Fred was an elderly man in the church. For years he had been a leader. He served on the Board. Now in retirement, he faced the unexpected burden of his wife's failing health and financial stress. It simply cost too much to live. Moreover, no one seemed able to help.

He turned to alcohol for relief. It provided him with some time where his mind was free from thinking about his pain. He knew better, but persisted. His behavior changed. He became erratic and unpredictable. He seemed to be hiding something. His friends noticed the change in his life and behavior. They spoke to him. He insisted he was fine. We kept an eagle eye on him for more clarity in what was going on.

One night he did the remarkable. I was officiating at a communion service, preparing the people to remember the death of our Lord. While I spoke he moved to the front, distracting me and others from what we were seeking to do. Finally, he stood and approached me. I set aside my microphone and listened to him. He asked to speak to the congregation. I sensed in him that this was the time he wanted to come clean.

With tears, he confessed before his friends of thirty years that he was an alcoholic. He had been living a lie. He would resign from his leadership roles, and seek help. He called it sin. He took responsibility. He tore off his mask and phoniness and told them who he was. The church rallied to his aid.

I went with a few of his friends to see him the next day. Both of these men loved him deeply. We found him lying in bed, having drunk himself into a sleep the night before. These two men admonished him. They stood up against his anger. They told him they would not go away. They were there to stay. After an hour, he broke again. They met with him often, supported him, and helped him.

He was freed. Moreover, none of this would have happened if he lived with private repentance because he did not want to shatter his image with others.

Great transformation takes place when we cease to live a lie. This should not surprise us. Lies are of the essence of sin. Think back to the story of original sin.

> Then the eyes of both were opened, and they knew that they were naked. And they sewed fig leaves together and made themselves loincloths. . . . the LORD God called to the man and said to him, "Where are you?" And he said, "I heard the sound of you in the garden, and I was afraid, because I was naked, and I hid myself." He said, "Who told you that you were naked? Have you eaten of the tree of which I commanded you not to eat?" The man said, "The woman whom you gave to be with me, she gave me fruit of the tree, and I ate (Gen. 3:7–12).

What is the immediate reaction of Adam and Eve to their sin? They covered up. They pretended to be fine. Pretense and hypocrisy are our greatest defense against admission of sin. Walking with Christ is called walking in the light!

There are objections: What about the scandal to the church? Isn't this airing dirty laundry, a prurient interest in people's private lives? Granted we live in a voyeuristic culture, we must be careful not to expose for exposure sake.

Genesis actually gives us guidance here. God did not ruthlessly expose Adam and Eve. He did clothe them. However, it was God who covered their sin and not them. We do not unnecessarily expose and humiliate. This violates Matthew's direction.

We know it is painful. I have had men in my leadership team ask if there was some other way. They felt it was shaming to the church and painful to the saints to see the soft underbelly of sin in the body of Christ.

The passage gives us no permission to delegate these steps to the elders. The requirement is not for professionals to do the admonition, but for the fellow believer, the brother or sister. The end is for the whole church, the members in covenant with each other, to hear the story. Yes, it is scandalous, humiliating, and painful. However, it is the way of Christ and the Spirit.

The elders may guide the process once it moves beyond the personal. It is crucial that the facts be confirmed, that there be opportunity for a fair hearing. Reputations are precious to God. In our psychological society, the desire to read between the lines is strong. Every one stumbles, but not all stumbling is worthy of censure. The elders must protect the church against slander as well as against other sin.

Our precious public image becomes too important to us. We struggle deeply with sin but don't want anyone to know. Everyone thinks we are doing fine. In public confession, there is a strong statement: I am not fine. I am a stumbling believer. I am living a lie. Sometimes there needs to be repentance for hypocrisy as well.

Full Exposure

The church must determine what its reputation is to be. Are we communities of perfect people whose image is based on some kind of flawless lifestyle? Alternatively, are we communities of reality, that face our problems squarely and with grace, and show that sin is taken seriously among us. The first creates hypocrisy and fear. The second creates a community of openness and helping. It also brings repentance from sin in those who hear.

What about loss of face? Having worked among face-saving people, I know the power of avoiding any words or actions that dishonor another. I have a simple question: What about saving the face of God? What about his honor? In face-saving cultures, we must obey Scripture rather than culture. The world of the New Testament was very sensitive to shame. Yet Paul calls the Thessalonians to act in a way that shames! The reputation of God and Christ is more important than the reputation of individuals or families.

A friend of mine has battled with abuse of alcohol for years. His cycle of returning to drink is about two years. When I met him, he had come to me for help. He was in a church where people did not expose their sin to anyone. He could not find anyone who would be his brother on the journey.

To make a long story short, he relapsed multiple times. I stood with him in the emergency room a number of times. I chewed him out and prayed with him too. Finally, he attended a treatment center. While he was there he attended a church that had a "recovery service." The pastor stood up and began the time by confessing his sin, acknowledging his need of the grace of God, and then they moved into worship in song.

When he told me about this, I thought, "All church services should be recovery services. Why do we need some special event for people struggling with sin?" We are sinners in need of the Gospel. Why the pretense?

I can only think of one reason: we are self-righteous and proud. We worry too much about our reputation and not enough about our sin. We have made our leaders into idols. We think of them as flawless. How wonderful it would be to nurture a congregation where pretense was abhorred and sincere and humble transparency was part of the life of the fellowship.

8

Repentance: The Gift of God

*He must learn and the church must learn that
Christian fellowship means a whole lot more
than hobnobbing with the saints. It means
sharing together the righteousness of Christ,
knowing communion in the spiritual joys and
battles of daily living.*

John White & Ken Blue

* * * * *

The goal of all this is repentance. It is that simple.
We are seeking to win our brother or sister. We want
them to listen to us, to the two or three, to the church.
If they listen, we have won our brother. If they refuse
to listen, we proceed to the next level of exposure.

What do we mean by repentance? How do we
know they have listened? Is it that simple? Are there
deceits and maneuvers along the way?

Let's start with a pastoral definition of
repentance. There are two components to it:

1. Repentance is taking full responsibility for the sin.

2. Repentance is turning from the idol we serve to the true God.

Repentance is throughout the Scriptures. The prophets called it "turning" or "returning" to Yahweh. Jeremiah put it this way:

> Go, and proclaim these words toward the north, and say, "' *Return, faithless Israel*, declares the LORD. I will not look on you in anger, for I am merciful, declares the LORD; I will not be angry forever. *Only acknowledge your guilt, that you rebelled* against the LORD your God and *scattered your favors among foreigners* under every green tree, and *that you have not obeyed my voice*, declares the LORD. *Return, O faithless children*, declares the LORD; for I am your master; I will take you, one from a city and two from a family, and I will bring you to Zion. And I will give you shepherds after my own heart, who will feed you with knowledge and under-standing.
> (Jer. 3:12–15; my italics).

Here Yahweh defines repentance as acknowledging sin, and leaving their false gods. He tells them the specific sins they have committed. The picture is one of an adulterous wife leaving her paramours and coming back to her husband. Obviously, the husband would not consider it repentance if she came back but kept a picture of her lover on her dresser. There is confession and forsaking involved in repentance.

Here we find it again in Hosea:

> Take with you words and return to the LORD; *say to him, "Take away all iniquity*"; accept what is good, and we will pay with bulls the vows of our lips. Assyria shall not save us; we will not ride on horses; and *we will say no more, 'Our God,' to the work of our hands.* In you the orphan finds mercy".
> (Hos.14:2–3; my italics).

The prophet says there must be words of confession and a repudiation and turning from the false gods being pursued. Multiple other passages speak to the same, but one of the clearest is Proverbs 28:13: "Whoever conceals his transgressions will not prosper, but he who confesses and forsakes them will obtain mercy." We do not hide our sin; when we repent, we expose it.

What do we mean by idols? How does that tie into sin? Sin is not just a transgression of a law of God. It involves a turning from God in unbelief and a turning to something else as "god." When I sin I am saying to God, "I do not trust you. I do not believe your way is good and best. I do not believe you are wise."

In place of the true God I worship pleasure, a lover, a lie, my money, a career advancement, my reputation, etc. Jeremiah speaks to the psychology of sin so clearly.

> for my people have committed two evils: they
> have forsaken me, the fountain of living waters,
> and hewed out cisterns for themselves, broken
> cisterns that can hold no water (Jer. 2:13).

We cannot worship God and sin. We cannot sin without worshipping idols.

Deep in the heart of man there is a powerful pull of idolatry. We want to worship this other god because of the pleasure it brings us. That love for sin and our false lover can actually keep us from repentance.

> Their deeds do not permit them to return to
> their God. For the spirit of whoredom is within
> them, and they know not the LORD (Hos. 5:4).

Now, let me become controversial. I believe it is burdensome to turn repentance into a once-for-all-time act. When we say "repentance is a determination not to sin again," we may imply that sinlessness is the result. Moreover, the failure to continue in obedience is a mark of false repentance. If this were the case, we would be done repenting once we had truly repented of every known sin.

I believe repentance is existential in most cases. For daily sin, repentance is "in the moment." When I tell a lie and repent of it, I am not saying "I will never lie again." You may not judge my repentance as false if I lie again. No, I am repenting of that particular sin. I tell my golf partner I took a five on a hole, when I know I took a six. That is a lie. Later I repent, "I told you a lie. I took a six there."

That is real repentance. This does not apply to conversion! There repentance and faith is a once-for-all act, empowered by the Spirit, resulting in a new creation.

If we cultivate the "once for all" mentality in a church, we will produce introspective and discouraged members. People who stumble into sin will become discouraged, thinking that they must not have meant it when they repented of that same sin the day before.

When I am seeking the repentance of a brother or sister in church discipline, I am seeking their repentance for a particular sin. This is why we need daily mutual admonitions to keep us on the path of walking in the light. Matthew 18 is applied every day. We watch over each other and encourage each other daily.

Now what are the deceits of our hearts that show repentance is false? There is worldly repentance. Paul spoke of it:

> ...godly grief produces a repentance that leads to salvation without regret, whereas worldly grief produces death. For see what earnestness this godly grief has produced in you, but also what eagerness to clear yourselves, what indignation, what fear, what longing, what zeal, what punishment! At every point you have proved yourselves innocent in the matter (2 Cor. 7:10–11).

Let's break this up. First, there is a distinction between the true and the false when it comes to feelings. Worldly repentance seems to be sadness for the consequences. It is a regret that one's pride has been damaged. It is sadness that people have been hurt. However, if the truth be told, you would do it again if you could control the circumstances. True repentance hates the sin as God hates it and accepts the consequences as part of the fruit of the sinning. The real thing is zealous, and full of indignation against sin.

Mike always showed up twenty minutes late for appointments. He finally confided that he could not drive to the church without going by an adult bookstore, and he was driven to stop and look. He could not control himself. He hated his sin and he was struggling with his sin. We talked about repentance. He needed a plan of attack. It was simple, he would drive another way. He would not place himself in the path of temptation. He refused. This was not repentance.

We may also say that worldly repentance may involve only feelings of sorrow. False repentance is like hating the effects of poison while continuing to drink it. It is weeping as one fires a gun repeatedly into an unfaithful spouse. This is not to say that there is no grief in true turning. No, tears of remorse are appropriate. Peter wept bitterly. He did more than that.

Then we may also say that worldly repentance is repentance without turning to the cross. Sometimes our repentance is really a form of disappointment with ourselves. We determine to try harder, or we give up in despair. Judas grieved for his sin and refused to run to Christ. Peter wept bitterly and came to Jesus. Judas destroyed himself because his ego had been ruined. Peter was humbled and found relief at the cross.

Another distinction is this: True repentance assumes responsibility without excuse, the phony kind makes excuses. One of the hardest parts of real turning from sin takes place when others were involved and they sinned too. It is so easy to want to shift some of the blame to them, or to wait for their confession.

"I have sinned." This is the essence of repentance. I see my self and my actions as God sees them. I have offended God. He sees what no one else sees. He abhors my sin. He grieves for my sin. It is fully my responsibility. No one made me do it. I cannot blame circumstances, genetics, or family. However, there are many confessions that are not quite repentance.

Pharaoh said he had sinned, but he qualified it. Saul the King said he had sinned but he made an excuse. We do the same today.

Sometimes we may say, "I am struggling with this sin." Now I am noble. This is the shift of doing lip service to repentance. Most of the right words are there. They admit it is sin, which is wrong, but they want to talk about struggle. Struggle gives them an excuse for sin.

Somewhere between an understanding of the power of indwelling sin and a perfectionist theology lies the path of repentance. I cannot end the power of the flesh. It will always set its desires against the Spirit. However, I may forsake the sin. I may have a holy determination not to sin. I must develop a plan to put the sin to death and not feed it further. Repentance requires a plan of attack: how will you put this sin to death?

Our psychological world has determined that explanation is everything. We can now discover the many factors that make us behave as we do. We understand ourselves; we now know why we do what we do. When we offer explanation we are asking people to "be nice to me, I have a tough road in life."

While the influence of environment is not dismissed in the Bible, it is not an excuse for sin. The deceit pattern of the patriarchs is passed from lying Abraham to the favoritism of Isaac to the cunning of Jacob. Nevertheless, it is all sin. We have a corrupt root, but we are accountable. Again, once we understand, what is the plan of attack?

There are so many more ways we shift blame, minimize the sin, resist specific actions for ceasing the sin. Words alone are not repentance.

Another distinction has to do with action. There is a fruit to repentance. If someone turns, they also stop doing what they were doing. I was part of confronting a man who was reported as involved with a mistress. She is the one who brought the report. She wanted out. She was being used, kept by him for his own purposes.

He freely admitted to the sin. It surprised us all. However, he absolutely refused to stop. As a matter of fact, he insisted he was practicing the virtue of honesty. He told us the truth! He thought he was spiritual for doing this. This was confession without repentance.

We discovered how unrepentant he was soon afterwards. He was a leader in the church. His marriage was in ruins. We pressed him for repentance. We gave him forty-eight hours to face his sin or we would begin the process of discipline by telling his wife. He flew into a blind rage. He accused us of being heavy handed. He slandered us as he left the church. He somehow confessed to his wife and turned her against us. He admitted he was wrong but he was not repentant.

Here is one of the most telling marks of unrepentant hearts: anger. Anger is the most frequent answer to rebuke. Anger can become hatred. Anger can spread to friends and family. Anger is a form of denial and evasion.

Repentance may appear genuine for a while and then fade. True repentance for a particular act endures. I like the picture of foam rubber. When you apply pressure to it, it changes shape. Release the pressure and it returns to the same form. This is repentance that lasts a very short while. Paul said the Corinthians were zealous to clear themselves. I have seen the contrast.

An intercepted e-mail gave a strong hint of an immoral relationship. The man who discovered the possibility went immediately to the parties involved. He confronted, gave them 48 hours to take the initiative and face their sin before an elder. One of them came the next day – with tears, and body-wrenching sobs, with shame and disgrace. He confessed. He begged for forgiveness. He faced the consequences. His feelings seemed genuine. We established a team to assist him in prayer and accountability.

After their first meeting, the repentance seemed less genuine. The man had lost some of his submissive spirit. He was taking over the process, telling the team what he would and would not do. Weeks later, it came unglued. His repentance was short-lived and insincere. His sorrow was the sorrow at being caught, not the sorrow at offending his God.

Contrast this story with that of a couple who began to attend our church. They seemed very shy, grateful for any attention given. One day they came to see me. Ten years before, they had rebelled against the Lord. Their marriage was started with adultery and divorce of their previous spouses. God had tried to stop them, sending various friends along their path when they were pursuing their romance. They ran from them all. God stopped their wedding when the pastor found out they were under the discipline of their former church. They went to a justice of the peace instead.

Then came repentance – deep, sorrowful repentance. They saw their rebellion and sin clearly. They were amazed at the chaos their actions had created in their families. They came asking for help. They took full responsibility. They blamed no one else. They were not angry. They did not minimize their sin.

We laid out a path of confession to all who had been offended. It was a long list. They went to each of them within a week. They went back to their former church, confessed, and asked forgiveness. They stood before our body as we sought to be their restoring fellowship. Nothing deterred their desire to clear themselves.

Two years later that desire was put to the test. At lunch I mentioned to one of their former church friends that we had them among us, that they had passed every test of repentance. He noted there was one more. It was one few knew about, one more offended party to be addressed. I made the call to Bill when I got back to the office. I explained. He understood. By the end of the day he had gone to that person as well.

Another way we repent is by facing the consequences of our actions and making restitution. Sometimes money must be returned. Apologies may need to be made. Sometimes the sin involves a breach of trust. There was sin and lies were told as well. Deception was frequent. The question then becomes: Where there has been sin that breaks trust, does repentance and forgiveness mean that trust is restored? This question arises especially in cases of marital infidelity. The spouse has admitted their sin, their adultery, and their deception. Is there now an automatic reboot to marriage before the trust was broken?

It is important to distinguish between trust and forgiveness. Forgiveness is free. Trust is earned. We are not supposed to trust everyone. That is the way of the fool in Proverbs.

As we shall see with sin and church leaders, trust is not the same as forgiveness. We cannot confuse the two. Forgiveness deals with debt and obligation. It releases the other from payment for their sin. There is no longer alienation.

Trust is based on character. It takes the relationship to a new level: confidence in integrity and character. Trust means I feel safe with this person. It is based on truth. It is earned.

Trust is eroded by sin, but more so by deceit and lies, disloyalty and gossip. Forgiveness can be given in an instant. Trust is re-earned over years. The first step in building trust again is confession: my words must match truth. However, that pattern must continue. It is not the same to ask for forgiveness as to ask for trust.

True repentance faces the loss of trust as a consequence for the lies told. True repentance faces everything that sin has brought and works its way back into the community.

Finally, perhaps the most subtle shift from true repentance is the person who is a quiet rebel. They confess and then demand forgiveness. They believe that their confession absolves them from all consequences. They blur the distinction between forgiveness and trust. They undermine the process of discipline by acting like victims of injustice. Sometimes rebellion is overt. Sometimes it is subtle. It is not repentance until there is taking full responsibility for one's sins and accepting all consequences as deserved.

Suppose we have admonished according to Scripture and they have responded? What do we do when repentance comes? If it comes after the personal admonition, after the two witnesses, or after the church speaks? It is a high privilege to be part of that work of God. James 5:19–20 says:

> My brothers, if one of you should wander from the truth and someone should bring him back, remember this: Whoever turns a sinner from the error of his way will save him from death and cover over a multitude of sins.

Jesus says there is great joy over a sinner who repents! Take them to dinner. Buy them a gift. Take along the two or three who helped. Celebrate with the whole church if it has come to them. We did.

One of the most agonizing experiences of church discipline I have had was with Julie. She and her husband were new to the church. We sought to welcome them to the church and the community. My wife and I had them over for dinner and introduced them to others. I remember hearing his testimony and wondering about its lack of clarity.

A few months later I arrived at the office early one Friday. Julie's husband was waiting for me. After a night in the car to think about it, he told me he was leaving his wife and son. I spent the next hour seeking to win his repentance. He would not listen to my pleas. He left my office, drove home, woke up his two-year-old son, and told him he would never see him again. Then he told his wife he was leaving. He would never come back. He had found the woman he loved and regretted the mistake of marrying Julie.

We went through the process of Matthew 18 with him. It was aggravating because he would not respond and he was hard to locate. We surrounded her with some godly women who gave of themselves in time and prayer and finances. She worked her way out of the pit of poverty and misery. It took years. They persisted in support through the whole process.

Six years later she became erratic in attendance. She seemed remote. Some of her good friends drew her out. Finally, she admitted there was a man in her life. They met at a picnic. He was kind and supportive to her and her son. They dated. After a few months she decided to move in with him. He was not a believer but as nice as any Christian. They would get married in a few months.

How heart wrenching it was to direct her support group to admonish her for her sin, then to hear the report from the Board member who went with them to confirm the facts. Sadly, after much pleading, waiting, and praying, we told the church. Since she did not respond, she was removed from our membership.

A year later, at a weekend of prayer and renewal, the body gathered at the Lord's Supper. We sat with the table in the middle of a large circle. It was a time of prayer and worship. There was no hurried pace, but a lingering before the Lord. I looked up, in the candlelit room, and spied Julie enter through the side door and sit alone in the back. She did not move or look up. I kept trying to get her eye, to make sure it was her. It was.

When I stood to conclude the service I told the church, "As we have sat here tonight I have seen God work in many of you. However, I have also seen a reason for amazement at God's patient love. A year ago one of our own family refused to repent of their sin. We obeyed the Lord and removed her from our membership. She was a prodigal, wandering in rebellion in a far country. We have prayed for her to come home. I will only ask her this: if she is here tonight because she is ready to come home, would she come up here with me."

She rose, and walked to the center of the circle. She wept as she came – loud sobs. When her closest friend saw her they came and walked with her. I asked her if she was turning from sin and wanting to be received back into the fellowship of the church. She answered in the affirmative. I asked the body if they would welcome her back home. They stood at once, saying "Amen!" applauding (the Lord, for joy), and weeping. We prayed for her, sang together, and rejoiced at the return of the Prodigal child.

This is the fruit we hope for from our obedience. This is the effect of a transforming community.

9

When Credible Faith is No Longer Credible

*The power of the church towards its members
may be referred unto three heads:
1. The admission of members into its society;
2. the rule and edification of them that belong
unto it;
3. the exclusion out of its society of such as
obstinately refuse to live and walk according
unto the laws and rules of it*

John Owen

* * * * *

At this point in the project, it should be clear that
membership in a local church is a holy matter. It
involves the clear testimony of faith in Christ and
the rule of Scripture through the Gospel to
accomplish the purpose of Christ in individuals and
the church. This is not often understood.

A few years ago one of the flock came to me
with a troubled expression written on their face.
They had just been finalizing their funeral

arrangements – one of those prepaid "deals" available in the USA. When they called back to their hometown in New England, they discovered that the cemetery of the church of their parents did not allow any one but a member to be buried there. They were no longer members. Their names had been removed from the roles twenty-five years before, five years after they left the area.

Church cemeteries were an old custom, long since forgotten. However, their parents and grandparents had been interred there. They were upset, "Who gave them the right to drop my membership?"

I queried them: Were they a member with us? (Yes.) Did they see any problem with being a member in two places? (No, why is that a problem? They belong to two health clubs.) It became apparent that they had no idea of what was involved in membership. After some explanation they assured me they had never thought of it that way.

This is not uncommon. Uninstructed saints see the local church as a place to hear a good sermon and make a few friends, a place with activities for their children. If that is all it is, then membership is not a serious commitment. Moreover, if it is not, certainly church discipline is ridiculous. If that were the case, "Mind your own business!" would be an appropriate response to someone dealing with my sin.

What is membership? Answering that question speaks directly to the nature of church discipline. Church discipline must be understood in light of the nature of the local church and its relation to the universal church.

When Credible Faith is No Longer Credible

Earlier I used this analogy to explain the local church: In the mountains where I live, there are large masses of roc, protruding from the ground. In the shifting of the earth's crust, gigantic slabs of stone shift through the softer soils and erupt on the surface. There is something much larger and invisible underneath. Local churches are "outcroppings" of the church universal. They are the places it shows up. Otherwise it is invisible.

There is no abstract or theoretical church in the New Testament. All churches are to be expressions of the deep and invisible work of Christ called the church. Being a member of a local church is to be under the oversight of the elders, joining with fellow believers to be an "outcropping" of the invisible church. This is not an option of the Christian.

So who is to be a member? The big donors? The children of members of long standing? Is it like a club where there must be recommendations and references to make sure they fit the rules and will not be disruptive?

The invisible church is made up of regenerate persons, who have trusted Jesus Christ as Lord and Savior. God knows the true members of the true church because he knows their hearts. These are the communing members.

However, we do not know their hearts. Remember, as Gandalf warned Frodo, not all that glitters is gold. Wolves come dressed in sheep's clothing. Local churches are a mixed company. Therefore, in this life, there must be corrective discipline. Sometimes it must go to the entire church.

At the time of entrance, we are to exercise due diligence in discerning the genuineness of someone's faith. How can we preserve the integrity of the outcropping to the best of our abilities? It is not light responsibility to be careful in the admission of members to the church.

The elders of the church interview the prospective member to discern the orthodoxy and credibility of their profession of faith. When words and life coincide in a reasonable manner, the person becomes a member. That is the front door.

Only when we understand the front door does the exit door make sense. There will be some who are not true believers. They will enter local churches. Over time they may prove themselves false. Not every sin is a denial of the faith. People will sin, but we speak to each other when there is sin. We call each other to follow Christ.

Sometimes sin is persistent and stubborn. Repentance is refused. Matthew 18 is the answer to the question: What do we do when a member denies their profession of faith by words or actions?

We have traced the careful process Jesus outlines. What appears to be a simple series of steps is rooted in the Mosaic Law. Careful protection of the person's reputation is mandated. Facts must be investigated. Slander must be avoided at all costs. No action may be taken where the evidence is unclear. The goal is their repentance. If they repent there should be great joy. However, what if they do not turn from their sin?

Now they must be removed from the membership. This is so much more than cleaning up the rolls. It is removing an apparent cancer. Jesus says:

> if he refuses to listen even to the church, treat him as you would a pagan or a tax collector. (Matt. 18:17).

I know there is great debate over what is meant by "pagan" and "tax collector." I do not think Jesus is saying we should treat them poorly. I think he is saying that we should no longer consider them a believer. This is the authority of the church, acting according to the Word of Christ (Matt. 18:18).

They come into the fellowship of a local assembly based upon a credible profession of faith. They are removed when the evidence of their lives or words makes their profession incredible.

This will seem unreasonable to many. The American scene has seen the development of a new notion of conversion. People are encouraged to "pray to receive Christ." If they say the right words, they are told this is faith. They have eternal life. They are secure. If they then become atheists or leave the church and never come back, we can know we will see them in heaven. Is this saying they can lose their salvation? Some will wonder, "Who are we to judge them?" Didn't Jesus tell us not to judge?

This is such a sad misunderstanding of the nature of Christ's work, saving faith, and

conversion. Faith is a turning from idols and a
leaning upon Christ for salvation. The weight of
the New Testament evidence indicates that Jesus
accomplishes something in people who trust in him
as Savior. Yes, he imputes his righteousness to them.
That is not all. He changes them. Listen to the
words of Paul:

> Do you not know that the unrighteous will
> not inherit the kingdom of God? Do not be
> deceived: neither the sexually immoral, nor
> idolaters, nor adulterers, nor men who
> practice homosexuality, nor thieves, nor the
> greedy, nor drunkards, nor revilers, nor
> swindlers will inherit the kingdom of God.
> And *such were some of you.* But you were
> *washed,* you were *sanctified,* you were
> *justified* in the name of the Lord Jesus Christ
> and by the Spirit of our God.
> (1 Cor. 6:9–11; my italics).

This is transformation. They are a new creation.
There will be some evidence of this new life.

More than that, this notion of powerless
salvation ruins all cause for discipline and strips
Jesus' words of their meaning. If persistent and
stubborn sin is the basis for this judgment by the
church, then it is a judgment that reverses their
acceptance into the local fellowship. It is a
statement by the church that their profession of
faith is no longer credible. If they are believers no
matter what, then what is the point of excomm-
unicating them? Why would we then treat them as
though they are lost?

When Credible Faith is No Longer Credible

I have a rule in life: "believe what people do not what they say". I base that rule on this and many other passages. No, their actions speak louder than their words. Their profession of faith is undermined by a life of resisting the light. They are removed from the privileges of the fellowship. What does that mean?

This is a description of excommunication. The word is full of medieval inquisition. It defies the anti-authority bias of the modern world. It breaks through our hypocrisy and desire to divorce our private lives from our public character. Such a possibility does not exist in the church of Jesus.

It is a good word. It tells what happens. The church acts to remove the person from the communion of the church. They no longer share its common life in Christ, its fellowship in the Spirit, its gathering as the Temple of God. They are aliens to the people of God.

Membership in a local church is rooted in the dynamic of shared life in the Spirit. Communing members are born of God, and their fellowship is with the Father and with his Son, Jesus Christ. There are certain privileges that are part of membership in a church. This does not mean the right to vote. It means the right to share in the common life of biblical fellowship. Non-believers may attend, but they are outsiders.

When there is a member, who made a profession of faith, but now denies it by stubborn sin, discipline is to be applied. What does this look like in practice?

Transforming Community

The Apostles faced this head on and gave specific instructions. To the Corinthians Paul writes:

> I have written you in my letter not to associate with sexually immoral people – not at all meaning the people of this world...I am writing you that you must not associate with anyone who calls himself a brother but is sexually immoral or greedy, an idolater or a slanderer, a drunkard or a swindler. With such a man do not even eat. What business is it of mine to judge those outside the church? Are you not to judge those inside? God will judge those outside. "Expel the wicked man from among you". (5:9–13).

Paul is making clear the boundaries of authority in the church. We do not perform church discipline on the world. The world is made up of sinners and sinners act like sinners! We should not be surprised. No, we have authority to judge those in the church.

He describes this as a change in relationship. It is a severance of some sort. He tells them this, that if they treated sinning non-believers in the same manner as the way they are to treat sinning believers, they would have to leave this world.

To the Thessalonians he states the case differently:

> If anyone does not obey our instruction in this letter, take special note of him. Do not associate with him, in order that he may feel ashamed. Yet do not regard him as an enemy, but warn him as a brother. (2 Thess. 3:13-15).

Both passages use the same word (*suvanamig-numi*). It means to associate or mingle with. Paul specifies: do not eat with the person. He says the goal is to exercise proper judgment in the church.

I believe Paul is describing the severance of the person from the intimacy of life in a local church. In the ancient world, a meal together was a mark of close friendship and covenant. It was much more about relationships than food. The Lord's Supper is the high water mark of the church: we gather as members of the same family, under the same blood. The early church shared their homes with each other (Acts 2:44–6).

People ask: does this mean I cannot smile at them if I see them on the street? Does it mean I take them off my Christmas card list? I think the answer is simple: they no longer participate in the sacred and intimate gatherings that are part of your life as a church. In some cases this may mean a home group. In others an adult Sunday school class. It certainly involves certain gatherings at meals. It certainly involves the Lord's Supper. It may not involve Sunday worship. Depending on the size of the congregation, this can be a very non-intimate event. The relationship must show that it has changed.

A great problem here is that our churches have become social clubs. The depths of biblical fellowship are lacking. There is little of the glowing heart that comes from speaking to and admonishing each other in love with the Scriptures. We do not provoke each other to love and good works. We do not confess or reprove sin. The content of conversation between Christians differs little from the unbelieving. The only difference is that we refer to God when we talk about our sports interests (as in "The Lord sure gave him a great golf game").

Therefore, excommunication has little meaning. They will just go down the street and join the next religious club. This would be the equivalent of a married couple who never enjoy the deep communion and physical intimacies of marriage. They exist under the same roof, but they rarely talk and when they do there is no sharing of heart. Imagine the absence of impact if one of them decided to divorce the other.

To make church excommunication more significant, we must first make the church more significant in its life together. Let's ask, what does excommunication look like?

One church defines it this way in their policy:

> Church discipline has nothing to do with "shunning" a person. It involves first confronting in love and gentleness and, if unsuccessful, withholding fellowship. It is not rejection of a relationship but a change in the nature of a relationship. If a person under discipline is not factious or disruptive or a harmful influence, he is welcomed to attend all church meetings that are open to unbelievers with the exception of small groups that meet for the purpose of fellowship. The pastors may decide to abbreviate or eliminate the process of appeal for repentance if the sin

is especially notorious, or if the member proves to be factious, disruptive, or leading others into sin or error. In these cases, the pastors may ask church members to avoid all contact with an individual in order to mitigate his sinful influence. (Covenant Life Church, Gaithersburg, MD USA)

The tone is crucial. What is withheld is not *all* relationship, but the unique spiritual intimacies of being in Christ. There is no bearing of each other's burdens, no praying for each other, no serving each other with our gifts.

They are not an enemy. This can be forgotten. Having withstood the worst of angry sinners, I know how easy it is to take it personally. When you have been slandered and attacked, it hurts. Rebellious sinners backed into a corner do not come out smiling. They attack and bite.

It is crucial to remember that they are responding to Christ. We represent him when we speak to them. This, again, is the authority of the church when it acts according to Scripture (Matt. 18:18).

They are not rejecting us but Christ. It is part of the war. I am to remember to treat them as I would a brother. I suggest that if it is someone with whom there will be natural association in work, neighborhood, or school that the believer sit with them and explain that their sin is an issue. It is a barrier. Tell them you desire their repentance.

How do we tell the church? We live in societies where public defamation is criminal. People will sue for libel. How do we proceed? How can we be faithful to Scripture and wise as serpents?

First, it is crucial that the church have a public policy of dealing with membership. Whether that is a congregational act of approving them or a written report from the elders, it must be public. It should involve names not just numbers. It should include new members, deaths, deletions, and requests for transfer. When receiving is public, then discipline can be public without fear of reprisal. No court will rule against a church that has a coherent policy and follows it.

Second, the announcement to the church should be in the same context as all other matters of membership. If it is done quarterly at a congregational meeting, then that is when discipline should be faced. There is no need to be in a hurry.

Third, I believe in writing out what I am going to say and keeping it on record. This guards me against foolish words and a wrong choice of words. Take counsel on what to say. One of my greatest mistakes in ministry was a failure to get advice in a statement read to the body over a matter of discipline. Good counsel might have saved me months of conflict. However, I do not mail out the information or distribute my comments. Everything is done verbally and it is not recorded.

Fourth, I speak in generalities. I give a warning of the nature of the meeting agenda in advance. I ask non-members who are present to leave the room. At the meeting I introduce the matter by telling what we are doing and whom we are dealing with. I give a report of how the sin was addressed (as in Matthew 18) and what the response has been. I do not give great detail about the sin. I may say they have broken their marriage vows, or that they have disobeyed a specific command of God. This is not a soap opera. People do not need all the details. It may be appropriate to name the two or three witnesses and to ask them to read prepared statements.

Fifth, I do not answer questions from the floor. This is information only. I am asking the church to seek them and their repentance. If they have questions, they may speak to me in private. I assure them that the individual will have an opportunity for a fair hearing and that members may ask questions if they feel we are in error.

Sixth, after a reasonable time (usually a few months), I bring a report. If it is repentance we celebrate! If it is resistance, I review the facts and announce that they will be removed. The response I call for is usually not a vote, but a time of united prayer. I avoid the "vote" because obedience to God is not something we vote on.

I have found that addressing the sin publicly with enough information to satisfy people's sense of justice has the added benefits of killing rumors and causing others to repent.

Is there an exception? I believe there are exceptions to this public component. When the admonished sinner moves toward suicide, public exposure is not wise or right. When public exposure deeply hurts innocent parties, it may need to be mitigated. I know some will feel this is compromise. I must remind readers that the context of the process is justice and truth. Scripture says mercy glories over judgment. Mercy is consideration for human weakness. I have found that when the action taken clearly brings great harm to human life or innocent parties, it is to be channeled into other settings. The church represents Christ in all it does.

The elders need to move wisely. Each case is different. Remember, the goal is to display the beauty of Christ and his holiness as his people on earth.

When handled well, it ministers to the body. I remember one of the earliest occasions of dealing with discipline before the church. We had gone through the process very carefully. There was no repentance. I told the church in the morning that we would have some important family business to deal with that night. People came. At the end of the regular service, I asked visitors to leave. Then I took time to instruct on the process. I told the story of the particular sinning member. I took time to make it clear that we loved them. My whole tone was personal, not business-like.

One of the things I remember about that evening was that people left at peace though sad. They knew it was right. They had heard enough to know this was not arbitrary and that something had to be done. They felt they had been obedient to Scripture as a body. Most significant to me was one man, who came up at the end of the service in tears. He choked on his words, but finally was able to say, "Thank you pastor, for doing this the right way. This is what the church is supposed to be." Amen.

10

Restoration Beyond Repentance

Since the confession of sin is made in the presence of a Christian brother, the last stronghold of self-justification is abandoned. The sinner surrenders; he gives up all his evil. He gives his heart to God and he finds the forgiveness of all his sin in the fellowship of Jesus Christ and his brother. The expressed, acknowledged sin has lost all its power. It has been revealed and judged as sin. It can no longer tear the fellowship asunder.

Dietrich Bonhoeffer

*****

Our hope is for repentance. We long for the brother to listen and turn from his ways. This is the goal, hope, and prayer. Suppose there is repentance? What are we to do? We kill the fatted calf and hold a celebration! One church in our area actually did that. They had a church celebration. They acted out the truth that there is more joy in presence of the angels over one sinner who repents than over ninety-nine who need no repentance. Is this the end?

I would say that often we think so. I have stopped there. I have regretted this. Scripture goes further in dealing with sin in the church. We must restore them. There are many reasons for this.

First, repentance does not relieve the person of the consequences of sin. We cannot turn back the clock. Moses repented but did not enter the land. David repented but his house was brought to disorder by his sin.

Sometimes after the repentance there is financial chaos. Alternatively, a spouse may be left perplexed as to how to pull a marriage back together. We wade in to help them clean up the mess.

Related to this, repentance is the first step on the right road. There may be many more. The person may need guidance in guarding himself from the same sin.

Then we may speak of the person's humiliation. Public censure is devastating. It may become a burdensome shame that is hard to escape. People may still be awkward with them, uncertain of what to say.

There are more. Each situation is different. I liken this to the aftermath of a health crisis. Many elderly people have strokes. They are rushed to the hospital. Friends surround the family. Doctors offer their skills. They stabilize. After a few days they are sent home. Is that it? It most certainly is not. They have to change how they live. Their spouses need assistance. Nurses and physical therapists come to the home and teach the stroke victim how to walk again. They give them exercises to do. Others come and place railings in the shower or along hallways. All this helps with the aftermath of the stroke.

When someone sins, they are disciplined. Their sin must be significant enough to merit this attention. It will have aftershocks, even after repentance. In light of this fallout, what are we to do? Not surprisingly, Scripture gives direction in two passages.

The Corinthian church took out judgment on the sinning brother in their midst. He repented. Paul says the challenge is not over. He instructs the church to go the final step:

> If anyone has caused grief, he has not so much grieved me as he has grieved all of you, to some extent – not to put it too severely. The punishment inflicted on him by the majority is sufficient for him. Now instead, you ought to forgive and comfort him, so that he will not be overwhelmed by excessive sorrow. I urge you, therefore, to reaffirm your love for him...in order that Satan might not outwit us. For we are not unaware of his schemes. (2 Cor. 2:5-11).

Paul calls us to be mindful of a few truths. First, there is no further punishment once repentance is accepted. There must be repentance as defined earlier. After repentance, we come to the aid of the sinning member. This is a hard truth to practice. Personal pain and a sense of justice can take over.

Suspicion may rule. If there is reasonable evidence of repentance, Paul says we are called to forgive and strengthen the repentant.

In history there has been a practice of putting the repentant on probation. A series of steps had to be taken to prove their repentance. This developed into the Catholic doctrine of penance. I understand this concern. Initial repentance is tested over time. However, this can dishearten the broken-hearted.

I once stood with a man who confessed his sin to the church. He made a clean confession, no excuses. The congregation affirmed their commitment to forgive and restore. Within three months he had turned on us in anger.

His anger was rooted in his sense of being on probation. He said we dropped him as soon as he confessed his sin too. There he was left with the chaos created by his sin and no one stood with him to help.

I do not believe in probation. If there are not sufficient grounds to believe it is repentance, then forgiveness should not be given. If there is, there should be no probation.

Highly theologically driven churches often become guilty of casuistry. We create long lists for measuring the reality of repentance. By our own standards we would have to admit we couldn't know if we have repented. Paul says: forgive and comfort.

His reasoning is clear. Failure to do so can overwhelm a person with sorrow. They have been stricken in their conscience with the vileness of their sin. They wonder if God will ever receive them back as a full son. They assume they will be on endless probation, a second-class citizen. Their conscience is tender. When the church, acting on behalf of Christ, fails to "loose" them, they take it as the act of Christ himself. Their hope of usefulness is dashed.

Paul also warns of Satan's devices. The devil is the accuser and the slanderer. He throws accusations against our conscience. He maligns us. We do not wish to join him in his work.

Instead, says Paul, reaffirm your love for that person. I believe this is where we fail. We forget that forgiveness is not enough. We are awkward with them and not sure what to say. Paul says: assure them of your love. Do it repeatedly. This man or woman is learning to walk again after a self-inflicted injury to their soul. They need support and help along the way as they regain confidence in their muscles. This includes everything from personal meetings for encouragement and prayer, to financial support for counseling.

What a wonderful ministry the church may have. The unrepentant cut themselves off from the gift of God to their souls. The repentant receive the full measure of grace present in the local assembly.

Elsewhere Paul uses the word "restore" to describe the role of the church:

> Brothers, if someone is caught in a sin, you who are spiritual should restore him gently. But watch yourself, or you also may be

tempted. Carry each other's burdens, and in
this way you will fulfill the law of Christ
(Gal. 6:1–2).

Plenty has been written on this notion. It means
to mend a net to make it useful, to set a bone that
has been broken. There is much involved. It is part
of the oversight of the flock. God is the model of
the care of souls:

> I myself will tend my sheep and have them lie
> down, declares the Sovereign LORD. I will
> search for the lost and bring back the strays.
> I will bind up the injured and strengthen the
> weak... (Ezek. 34:15–16).

To restore means to give consistent time to the
person. Over the years I have developed a plan.
First, I meet with the person monthly. This is to
keep up my role of shepherd. I encourage, probe and
support. I ask the spouse to join us if there is one.
Sometimes we neglect the children. We must not.

Next, I establish a restoration team. This is a
team of qualified friends who meet with them
weekly in person and are in touch via phone or e-
mail the rest of the week. These men or women
need to be godly, good listeners, well-established
in their own spiritual habits. They must be
committed for at least a year and available weekly.
I train them and keep up with their activity.

1. The goal of the team is to listen, to encourage, to guide them in making restitution,

and to call them to submission to God each week. They want to help the repentant make a complete assessment of the path of sin they took and what they need to do to flee from it in the future.

2. They should help them re-establish spiritual disciplines, especially the daily putting to death of sin and honest admission of sin. They can study a book together. Books in godliness are a great help here.

3. They need to meet where they can pray over the person. I believe James 5 comes into play here. They are confessing their sins and being prayed for so that they may be healed. They need to have authority to help the person financially. They need to report periodically to the elders.

4. They need to meet for at least six months. The process of facing the consequences of sin, rebuilding one's life, and establishing a new record of accomplishment takes time. This is not to question their repentance. It is admitting there are consequences. Bad habits have been established and must be broken. Godly habits need to be established.

This does not mean the person being restored simply returns to their previous work in the church. No, they are in a process of being restored because they have disqualified themselves from office. I recommend they refrain from all ministry until the process is complete and they are stable.

All this needs to be spelled out in writing and agreed to. Vagueness does not serve anyone. Dates and times and schedules must be on the calendar. Expectations must be clear. Unwillingness to close on clarity may be a mark of residual pride.

The hope is that they will be able to walk with the Lord again, without undue shame. The goal is for them to become a healthy member of the local church, useful to others in serving them.

I believe that they need to remain in the flock. Every bone of their bodies will want to flee from embarrassment. They will argue that they need a fresh start. The church may resist having them there. However, it is essential and healing to live with the truth about what they have done and to rebuild a reputation with those who know the facts.

It will be the painful facing of the effects of their sin. It will also be a deep experience of the love of the saints that will create a deep cleansing of their lives. I would not work with anyone in restoration if they were not weekly attendees in the public worship of the church. Trust has been breached and must be rebuilt by integrity.

I have seen so many examples of people who began the process of rebuilding their world and life, only to fail because of lack of support. It is a painful lesson of twenty years of ministry that follow through must happen. The results can be so varied unless we restore. When we follow Christ, beauty emerges from the ashes.

Early on in pastoral work, I was part of a church where a leader was found to be engaged in repeated acts of adultery. He had not come forward to confess this. He was exposed by one of the many women with whom he had had adulterous relationships.

We confronted him. He fell apart before us. He sobbed and groaned. Seventeen years of duplicity had been a great weight to carry. He submitted to the elders. He handed in resignation and gave up his ordination. He confessed to his wife and she forgave him. He was an elder, so we believed his sin was a public matter and required a public confession.

A few days later he stood before the church (more on that later) and confessed. People lined up afterwards to embrace him and his wife. He stayed in the flock. He came and worshipped each Sunday but rarely lifted his eyes from the ground. A group of men surrounded him, helped him with work and money, and met with him weekly. He spent time, at church expense, with a counselor. Eight months later we began to see a change. He looked up at worship. He smiled when he saw others. His repentance was deep. He faced every humiliation and accepted it. He denied every opportunity to teach or minister. Within a few years he was remarkably transformed.

The story is not always so encouraging, especially when no one offers to support and restore. A contrast was another leader, involved in sexual perversion. His position called for the same admonition. He repented. He handed in his ordination. He resigned. He stood before the church to confess. The people embraced him. He stayed in the flock.

However, no one met with him. No one strengthened his soul. People did not make time for restoring him. In a few months he had a growing despair. Six months later it was anger. He felt like he had been ignored. His charge was accurate.

There are dangers. First, the friends of the person being restored may become advocates for their cause and stir up support for them. This can lead to division. It must be clear that the matter of restoration rests in the hands of the elders or pastor. It will not be considered until their reputation for repentance is long term and evident to most. Even then, there will be a process for their being brought back into former responsibilities.

Second, there will be those who want to prolong the process or shorten it unduly. This will include the desire to make the process more severe or more lenient. In both cases it really becomes a matter of trusting the elders to act wisely. The elders must also keep an open door to people in the flock, for their questions. I believe all desire the person's full recovery. We must simply forbear with each other in the differences we may have in how we approach it.

This brings us to a point of controversy: Can a fallen minister be restored? What about an elder? What about a Sunday school teacher?

Each church has its own set of qualifications for certain responsibilities in the church. Some require only that the individual be a member in good standing, not currently under a disciplinary process. This may be true of the choir. Churches need to consider the qualifications necessary for each position of service.

There are other responsibilities and offices that require a reputation worthy of trust. Obviously, sin destroys that trust. It should. Some churches keep an immoral pastor after his repentance out of compassion. This cheapens his ministry and the church.

No, they need to rebuild trust. They need to prove their character once more. This is possible, but rare. Our next chapter considers such a process for someone brought back into the role of an elder or other office bearer in the church.

11

A Process for Restoration

*I believe the tempter has gained as great victory
in getting but one godly pastor of a church to
neglect discipline as he has in getting the same
pastor to neglect preaching*

Richard Baxter

*****

In my twenty years as a pastor I have seen a growing
movement among churches – a movement to
restore sinning leaders to ministry leadership. It
began the first year I was a pastor. It continued
through some fairly public scandals where mega-
church pastors or parachurch leaders were found
morally unqualified. Some restorations have
integrity. Some are scandalous in their disregard
for church authority and the standards of the
Word.

Serving as an elder is more than a calling. It is
an earned trust. I serve because of character
qualifications established in my life by the grace of

God. Elders are those held in highest esteem within a local church. My authority is God given but character based. When character is lost I lose the trust of the flock. The honor of Christ is at stake in the integrity of the shepherds of the flock.

Paul makes very clear in 1 Timothy 3:1–7 what is required of elders:

> Here is a trustworthy saying: If anyone sets his heart on being an overseer, he desires a noble task. Now the overseer must be above reproach, the husband of but one wife, temperate, self-controlled, respectable, hospitable, able to teach, not given to drunkenness, not violent but gentle, not quarrelsome, not a lover of money. He must manage his own family well and see that his children obey him with proper respect. (If anyone does not know how to manage his own family, how can he take care of God's church?) He must not be a recent convert, or he may become conceited and fall under the same judgment as the devil. He must also have a good reputation with outsiders, so that he will not fall into disgrace and into the devil's trap.

What is Paul saying? Is he requiring some kind of perfect man to be an elder? This is not the case at all. He is speaking to reputation. He is saying that the leaders of the church need to be men known for these qualities. His standards were not uncommon to the ancient world. We want men who will be faithful to God and our souls as leaders.

A Process for Restoration

Ministry exposes people to many pressures. It is not honoring to Christ to treat qualification lightly. John Chrysostom speaks to this as clearly as any in the history of the church:

> The priest's shortcomings simply cannot be concealed. On the contrary, even the most trivial soon get known. The weakest athlete can keep his weakness secret as long as he remains at home and pits himself against nobody. So with other men: those who lead a retired and inactive life have their solitude as a cloak for their private faults; but when they are brought into public life, they are compelled to strip off their retirement like a garment and show everyone their naked souls by their outward movements.[1]

These criteria pose a question: If someone once met these criteria and has sinned their way out of that qualification, can they be re-qualified? In other words, is Paul telling us to look at their FBI file or their more recent record of accomplishment? Does one felony disqualify them for life or for a certain number of years? Does it depend on what sin is involved? Is this a matter of reputation for present character or a black mark in one's file over past sin?

I believe Paul is asking the church to look at the people who are known for these qualities. He is not calling them to investigate their histories as

---

1. Chrysostom, Saint John, *Six books on the Priesthood* translated by Graham Neville. St Vladimir's Seminary Press, Crestwood, New York, 1984.

Christians (I assume we understand that pre-conversion behavior is not at all an issue here). It means the church is to take its time to evaluate character. We are to look at a person long enough to know their character before we appoint them to eldership.

We do not carry our reputations with us either. Just because someone was an elder somewhere else does not mean they can import that respect into a new setting. No, they must earn that same trust in their new church. How are we to evaluate character? Should we have a statute of limitations in looking into someone's past? I think so. We need to know their record in recent years. However, the fact that they were divorced twenty years ago does not mean they cannot have rebuilt their godliness into being a one-woman man and a faithful leader of their home.

All that being said, it seems that certain sins have a way of holding themselves over a person for a lifetime. This is simply the way God has made us. If someone makes a mistake, we forgive them. If they deliberately lie to us and cover up, we may be slow to trust them again.

Great sin has a way of marring our souls. The Puritans called it a wounded conscience. I have known many occasions of men and women who, as a result of sin, were deeply motivated to prove themselves. They were overly sensitive to criticism and defensive under evaluation. Their godliness was not for God alone, but for their own egos and as atonement for their sin. This is a distorted motivation.

A Process for Restoration

That being the case, I still believe someone may re-establish a godly reputation among a flock where their sin was scandalous. It is simply fraught with dangers.

Before we answer that question, I want to put it in a larger context. Let's look at the process for dealing with sin in leaders, and how it differs from the process for members. Then we will consider how restoration may happen.

The process and principles for dealing with sin in elders is described by Paul. He writes to Timothy concerning elders:

> The elders who direct the affairs of the church well are worthy of double honor, especially those whose work is preaching and teaching. For the Scripture says, "Do not muzzle the ox while it is treading out the grain," and "The worker deserves his wages." Do not entertain an accusation against an elder unless it is brought by two or three witnesses. Those who sin are to be rebuked publicly, so that the others may take warning (1 Tim. 5:17–20).

The context is about leadership. He commends a faithful elder, and frees them to be supported by the church for their ministry. He then speaks to what to do when there are charges of sin against them. His instruction is two-fold.

First, elders are to be protected from mudslinging. An accusation against an elder is not to be heard unless supported by eye-witnesses. Why this special protection? The very nature of leadership is public visibility. As such it is subject to excessive scrutiny. This is what we call the "fishbowl." With scrutiny come gossip, malicious gossip, and false conclusions. Jesus, the sinless One, was subject to all of the above! Paul is essentially saying, "Don't believe what you hear and only half of what you see." Elders need protection but never blind loyalty. The Name of Christ is too important to tolerate immature or ungodly behavior in an elder.

Second, when there is eyewitness evidence or personal admission, Paul changes the rule for elders. The sin of elders is automatically to be confessed before the church. What does this mean?

In some cases it simply means that the scope of the transgression is equal to the scope of the confession. If I speak inappropriately of my wife while I am preaching, perhaps demeaning her, then I am to confess that to the people who heard me. If I make a decision that is a mistake and that decision is public, I must confess it. This wins trust!

Paul, however, is talking about something else. He is speaking of transgressions that disqualify from office. Such sin must be faced squarely. It cannot be swept under the rug. One church I know of, after discovering adultery in their minister, sent him on vacation and he never came back.

Sometimes the pastor will voluntarily make confession. At other times it will be a rebuke with the congregation and the rest of the elders receiving a warning from it. If it is disqualifying, it includes a resignation or dismissal.

A Process for Restoration

Some may hear this and think this is a disregard for people's honor and good name. As I have reflected on this over the years I would have to say that God has been exceedingly blunt about the sins of leaders in Scripture. Here is a quick list: Abraham's lies, Moses' anger, Samson's lusts, David's adultery, Peter's denial. God is more concerned for integrity than for our cherished reputation. A price of leadership is the loss of my status as a private citizen in the kingdom of Christ. I am a public person. When I sin is such a way that I am disqualified, I sin publicly.

Does it depend on what sin? Is all sin to be confessed? What about giving them a chance to start again? I certainly believe that some sin disqualifies an elder from holding office. Other sin disqualifies them from continuing where they are. The first violates the integrity of the role of elder, the second breaches trust or honor before fellow elders or a congregation. The former are matters of immoral behavior, greed, or patterns of anger – these lead to discipline. The latter may take place where there has been disloyalty, a lie, theft, or deceit – these lead to dismissal or resignation.

Now we come to our original question. Suppose this has happened. The elder has sinned scandalously. He is disqualified from office. He has made public confession. He has resigned his office and submitted to the other elders for restoration. A team of godly men has met with him for a year. His life, his marriage, his work are stable and strong again in Christ. Can this man ever be reappointed?

Since I believe that holding public responsibility in the church is a matter of proven character and earned trust I must hold out this possibility. I doubt it can occur fully in the same church where the disqualification took place. Forgiveness is much easier than trust. Some will always be skeptical of the restoration process.

I also believe that the very nature of the purpose of the atonement is restorative never exclusive. In John 21 Jesus re-established Simon Peter as Apostle after his denial. He did it by creating a scene just like his denial: fireside, three questions, using Peter's very words about loving Jesus more than the others. He did it at the seaside, where he first called Peter. In the end he re-commissioned Peter as leader of the Apostles. The price for Peter is two millennia of humiliation!

Jesus gave us a word to help us in developing a process for rebuilding reputation and taking on greater ministry responsibility. It is found in Luke 16:10:

> Whoever can be trusted with very little can also be trusted with much, and whoever is dishonest with very little will also be dishonest with much.

I believe the process of restoring someone to ministry should be the same as the process that took him or her there in the first place. It was one step at a time; proven faithfulness in lesser things brought greater responsibility.

When I was in seminary, many of the students flocked to a booming church nearby. We lined up and knocked on the door of the pastor to tell him we were his answer to the need for pulpit supply. He held a meeting with all the seminary students. He told us there were many opportunities for ministry. There were children to be taught and parking lots to be supervised. He asked us to prove ourselves faithful in small ways. Then we would be given greater tasks. He had a phrase: man does not seek a ministry, a ministry seeks the man. He was saying that character would be noticed by God and by other believers.

A friend needed help with this. His predecessor had moved on to a new church. There it was discovered that he had been adulterous with a woman in his previous flock, the one my friend now pastored. His current church stumbled through a process of discipline. They believed he needed to go back and make confession to the church where the sin had taken place. He did so. He resigned as pastor and moved back to that church, asking them to restore him. His repentance seemed real. His heart looked submissive. Now what?

We developed a plan together based on Luke 16. It had these steps:

1. It would begin with one year for meetings with a restoration team such as I have described above. At the end of that year, if they affirmed him, he would be given a role of servant ministry.

2.Servant ministry was a non-teaching role, such as custodial work or changing diapers in the nursery. He would serve in that capacity, without any responsibility for others, for a period of six months. If proved faithful, he would move to a responsibility of servant leadership.

3.Servant leadership involved responsibility for a larger task that required working with others but still did not involve a ministry of the Word. This may be nursery supervision. If faithful there for at least six months, he would move to servant teaching.

4.Servant teaching is a ministry responsibility where there is no public presence with the whole church, such as teaching children. Again, if faithful here, he would be given greater exposure and responsibility.

The pattern had clear criteria for evaluation. The team would continue to look at his life, marriage, family, and attitude. They would observe him at work. They would advocate his being given greater responsibility once he had been faithful where he was. The issue addressed in this process is any ego-driven motivation. These are behind-the-scenes roles. They are tests of character.

The process is a bit grueling, and deliberately so. Let me explain. Paul says we are not to lay hands hastily on others (1 Tim. 5:22). To appoint people to leadership too quickly makes us partakers of their sin when they fail.

There are pitfalls to avoid. I have seen restorations by virtue of "God called me to preach. I have repented. That is all that is needed." Such a path mocks the people of God and their need to esteem their elders for godly character.

I have seen restorations by the benevolence of the flock. They hear the confession, offer forgiveness, and refuse to accept the resignation. Pastors are beloved by most of their flock. Most people want to give their pastor the benefit of the doubt. This again misses the point. The office of elder needs to be esteemed, not just loved. In our postmodern days every standard is fuzzy. It must be clearly asserted that forgiveness is one thin and trust is another. Exemplary behavior is the foundation of trust in the office of an elder.

I have seen restorations without a process. They either fail for having no benchmarks or succeed without apparent reason. If a man fails when given a great responsibility, Jesus seems to be saying that he is not a faithful man. Restoration cannot be to give him the exact same responsibility without a process of re-establishing faithfulness.

There need to be measurements. If there are objective criteria it enables the elders and the church to have good reason to affirm or deny the person's taking on a role of elder again. If there is objectivity it gives great confidence to the restored.

What about less scandalous sins? There are sins which disqualify an elder or pastor from his office.

These result in his yielding his position and his ordination. There are sins which are less severe but break trust. I may err in judgment and confess it, but my error may be such that I have lost the confidence of people. It may be a repeated error.

I have grown to value the trust relationship between elders and between people and pastor. I have made the mistake of "covering" a sin in another, which was a violation of trust. This includes misuse of funds, breaking confidences, disloyalty in any public setting, or a lie. In every case, where trust was disrupted, it became a hindrance to all who were affected. Candor ended. Openness stopped. Confidence was eroded.

I believe, as a result of experience, that any significant break in trust requires the person to step down from their office or to find a new place of ministry. I do not believe this is a matter of forgiveness. Trust is based on proven reliability. If someone breaks trust, those affected have doubts in their hearts.

When my son was very young, he lied to me. It was not hard to prove his lie. As his father I wanted him to know how important trust is. I told him he could never lie to me again, because if he lied we could not be friends. I would never know if he was telling me the truth.

Elders and officers of the church serve based on trust, and work together based on trust. If that is lost, then there needs to be a surgical removal of the cause of broken trust.

A Process for Restoration

Moreover, what if there is no repentance? I have watched as an elder defied the right of the church to judge their sin. I have seen pastors play the part of repentance and inwardly seethe at the discipline. Angry sinners must be removed from the fellowship as quickly as possible. Those whose sin is public and repentance is unclear must be removed quickly. Their cancer may spread and people may come to their side if they linger.

Is it worth the effort? What I have described is a great deal of work. Family therapists would say it creates a dysfunctional system where large amounts of time are given to the unhealthy! While I understand the theory, I wonder what Jesus would say. He said that God is like a shepherd who leaves the ninety-nine to go after the one. Certainly the rebuilding of lives, which have fallen into sin, is the very essence of ministry. However, it must be done without crippling a church.

12

God at Work

It's very comforting for me to know that heaven supports me in the process of discipline, because people often think that if you try to confront sin and call it what it is, you are being unloving. But what you're really doing is fighting God's battle and lining up with heaven.

John MacArthur

* * * * *

As we come to a conclusion of the nature of church discipline I want to return to the glory of the church. The New Testament gives us a sense of such deep identification between Christ and his body that persecution of believers is persecution of Christ himself. When we work out these truths and seek to live the Gospel unto holiness, we are engaging in holy work.

Exercising church discipline is never pleasant. We ought to mourn as we remove a cancer. We certainly should shout for joy and dance when the wanderer comes home. However, I have done more than grieve and rejoice in discipline and restoration. I have stood in awe. There is a work of God in discipline that is wondrous and forbidding. This is not the mechanical exercise of policy similar to a legal or medical association disciplining a member for ethical error. No, God works, his presence is real.

Lest you think I am expounding my experience, let me cite references woven into the passages on discipline which reveal the same. Both cases show that church discipline is more than a human activity, even one done in obedience to Christ. We begin with part of the Matthew 18 passage. After laying out the process for believers to address sin in each other, Jesus speaks this promise:

> I tell you the truth, whatever you bind on earth will be bound in heaven, and whatever you loose on earth will be loosed in heaven.
> (Matt. 18:18).

The passage has been obscured by the debate of church history. Some see it as the keys given to the descendants of St. Peter. Others take it as a retroactive authority – i.e. Jesus has already done the act and we are following suit. Apart from the controversy it seems obvious that the Lord is defining his presence in the actions of the church.

Consider the context. Jesus addresses how the church is to address sin. He speaks of private rebuke, followed by the participation of confirmatory witnesses, and leading ultimately to censure and excommunication. The person is now considered to be lost. These are serious matters.

What Jesus is saying is simple. He is defining their boundaries. He does not give carte blanche to the church to do as it pleases and assume his blessing on all actions. This is a stern warning to churches not to abuse this principle and practice. The Lord of the church does not endorse discipline over silliness or petty sin. If someone is not having their quiet time, he is not with us in our censuring them. If they drive a red BMW, he is not for our rebuking them. We must be careful to make sure we are true to his written directions.

Jesus is giving a promise concerning a very specific situation: the maintenance of the integrity of the body of Christ. He is building his church and care must be taken in that process. When the church acts according to his will, as described in his Word, then he is at work in its actions. Consider it his hand working through the glove of the church.

It also seems obvious that the authority given would be similar to a government authorizing an ambassador to follow a certain set of guidelines in a treaty negotiation. The government says to the ambassador: "When you act in these guidelines, we stand with your decision completely. You represent us fully."

Here again we find the glory of the church. Of what other group can it be said that when they act, the Lord of the cosmos acts too? This interpretation actually establishes the basis for the other passages.

> When you are assembled in the name of our
> Lord Jesus and I am with you in spirit, and
> the power of our Lord Jesus is present, hand
> this man over to Satan, so that the sinful
> nature may be destroyed and his spirit saved
> on the day of the Lord (1 Cor. 5:4–5).

The Corinthians were tolerating sin in their midst, a case of incest. Paul calls them to judge the sin. He describes their gathering on the Lord's Day as an assembly in the name of Christ. He says Christ is present in power. This is remarkable. It almost seems understated. No attempt is made to explain it. It is understood. This is not how most understand the gathering of the church on Sunday!

This is similar to Matthew 18 — the promise of his ratifying authority and the promise of his presence where two or three are gathered. Even a small church is a church. The greater context of discipline is the presence of Christ.

The church is commanded to hand the man over to Satan. How are they to do that? Satan is a malevolent spirit. They are flesh and blood. Apparently Satan is present in the church as well and their actions put this man in the devil's hands.

The allusion may be to Job and his work to ruin that godly man, but Job was not under discipline. However, it is obvious that the New Testament assumes that the devil can work immediately upon the life of a professed saint. Perhaps it is their sin which gives him his toe-hold (Eph. 4:27).

The destruction of the flesh is ambiguous in that "flesh" has many meanings. Here it is contrasted with "spirit" and seems to refer to their physicality.

Here is a man, who once was subject to the Lord of darkness and under his malicious rule, now being given back to his hateful tormentor. I think Paul is saying, "Let him find out what his former master will do to him now."

Here is something amazing too. Satan will now work to accomplish the purpose of God. Again, Paul seems to assume they understand his thought without explanation. There is a spiritual component to church discipline that involves the world of demons.

Christ is present, the church has power to hand a member over to Satan, and Satan will accomplish the purpose of God by affecting the man's flesh. This may tie in with what follows in 1 Corinthians 11. Again, speaking to their lack of accurate judgment of their sin, he warns them:

> A man ought to examine himself before he eats of the bread and drinks of the cup. For anyone who eats and drinks without recognizing the body of the Lord eats and drinks judgment on himself. That is why many among you are weak and sick, and a number of you have fallen asleep. But if we judged ourselves, we would not come under judgment. When we are judged by the Lord, we are being disciplined so that we will not be condemned with the world
> (1 Cor. 11:28–32).

The Corinthians were abusing the Lord's Supper. They thought it was just bread and wine. No, says Paul, when you abuse the symbol, you abuse what it represents. Christ will not be blasphemed or disregarded. He will be holy in his body, the church. So, he judges them. Some of them are sick and a few have died. Their sin has so dishonored Jesus that he steps into the mess and acts. They may have explained this differently, but Paul is saying, "This is the hand of God in judgment."

Paul had warned them that God prizes his church, his temple. He warned them that God's judgment rests on those who destroy God's temple.

> Do you not know that you are God's temple and that God's Spirit dwells in you? If anyone destroys God's temple, God will destroy him. For God's temple is holy, and you are that temple (1 Cor. 3:16-17).

He is speaking there of the local church. This harkens back to the Old Testament. We are told in the Old Covenant of God's judgment on rebellious Israelites (Numb. 14, for example) or on defiling priests (Lev. 10). Both of these were judgments for despising God's holiness. In the New Testament, Ananias and Saphira serve as a reminder of the holiness of the church.

This is nothing more than the outworking of the glory of the church. It shows how deeply Christ is working in local assemblies. The seven churches of Revelation describe him as the one who walks among the candle-sticks. He is present. We are his people. He is jealous for his bride.

I have said that I am in awe of what happens in church discipline. I believe I have seen the truth of these passages worked out in the process. Almost every time we have engaged in church discipline to the final step I have seen the dreadful judgment of God over the individual who despised his rule and Word. Let me explain.

As I think on the various cases of discipline I have been part of or the stories I have heard from other pastors, a common pattern emerges. I used to think that when we disciplined members and they resisted, they would simply leave. That has not been my experience. An unseen hand seems to press into their lives. Sometimes they abandon themselves to sin.

Remember the pastor's wife who sinned and was faithfully admonished by her local church. Her refusal to repent was a headlong rush into sin. She turned from Christ and became immoral, including a lesbian relationship.

I saw a mild mannered man abandon his wife and move into series of adulterous and perverse relationships. He faced repeated broken marriages and personal wreckage.

How do I understand this? Paul says in Romans that God may judge by delivering people to their lusts. I believe that is what happens in church discipline. Christ acts, by the Spirit, through the actions of the church, to do just that.

The other tragic direction is the loss of health

and stability of mind. I have seen attempts at suicide, a tragic rejection of people who would have embraced them in repentance. Sin is, ultimately, a form of insanity. How else can I describe the intense anger and denial of all wrong-doing by someone caught in adultery? This was followed by accusations against others for their sin (I didn't do it and it's your fault that I did)! What about the man who, a year after being disciplined was scarcely recognizable to a member and friend of many years.

David noted that when he refused to confess the hand of God was upon him day and night (Ps. 32:3–4). He describes the misery of his soul in his sin (Ps. 38). James tells us that physical healing is often tied to confession of sin (Jam. 5:16).

God is not passive when his professed children make light of his honor and his Son. God is not always patient in his judgments. Moreover, often his judgments are what break the stubborn will of the offender. I have seen cases where he did so.

I recall a man, after ten years of stubborn denial of any guilt in his adultery and divorce, come to tell me he was now repentant. He described in detail the hand of God upon his life to try to stop his sin, the many occasions the Lord gave a door of escape when sin was luring him in. He had been pursuing another woman and she was gladly responding. They began to talk by phone every day and set up meeting places and times where they could see each other outside the gaze of friends. Almost every time they had a rendezvous, God sent someone they knew to that place to disrupt their pleasure. The one time I remember was their surprise at seeing someone from their church in a hotel lobby in a small town 500 miles from home.

They resisted God. In addition, when the church became aware of their sin, they resisted them. They divorced their spouses. The church excommunicated them. They moved to the other side of town and set out to get married. They made up a story to deceive a pastor and he agreed to marry them. The day of the wedding God sent someone to the pastor to tell him the truth. He confronted the couple and refused to do the wedding. They went to a justice of the peace.

After he had made his choice, ruined his family, and sinned against God, he found his inner world collapsing. While he thought he would be free, he was in a torturous anguish of soul. He would go into his backyard and sob with wails and groans. God would not go away. His misery increased for ten years. He gained weight. His enjoyment of life diminished. At last he broke. He was now ready to come clean. His repentance, to this day, was sincere.

I have wondered what would have happened in these cases if churches had not exercised the authority of Christ is dealing with sin in a godly way. Would there be a cleansing of the church? Would there be the hand of God in discipline? Would there have been repentance?

God's church is blood-bought. God's children are blood-bought. When a sheep wanders, the shepherd moves heaven and earth to bring it home.

The Father, Son, and Holy Spirit are fully involved in church discipline. Satan himself is used for their purposes. When we follow the command of Christ we are true partners with Him in his work.

13

Tough Calls: Public Offense

Reproof is unavoidable. God's Word demands it when a brother falls into open sin. The practice of discipline in the congregation begins in the smallest circles. Where defection from God's Word in doctrine or life imperils the family fellowship and with it the whole congregation, the word of admonition and rebuke must be ventured. Nothing can be more cruel than the tenderness that consigns another to his sin. Nothing can be more compassionate than the sever rebuke that calls a brother back from the path of sin

Dietrich Bonhoeffer

* * * * *

Of course, there are exceptions and cases that must be worked out differently right from the beginning. It is not that these are exceptions to the rule. Rather, these are opportunities to apply wisdom and discretion in a different way.

Most sin in the church is private. People sin in dark rooms or alone at a motel. They send in a false report on their taxes. No one knows. Our love of being respected as good would probably restrain us if we were considering a public sin. If we sin in less than private ways, it is "small sins."

When it comes to private sins Matthew 18 is enough to guide us and to protect reputation. However, humanity being what it is complicates matters. Some private sins become public because of rumor, gossip, and slander. Some are discovered and prosecuted. Some sins are public by nature. Paul agreed with this when he noted the distinction:

> The sins of some men are obvious, reaching the place of judgment ahead of them; the sins of others trail behind them (1 Tim. 5:24).

The elders of the church must be prepared to deal with public sins: a pregnant single woman, a scandalous action by a Christian publicized in the news, a contention between members, or an ungodly action that took place in a public setting.

I believe the simple rule is this: Deal with the sin as publicly as it is known. There are qualifications for this. Some sins are known by many through rumor. Some sins are to be covered in order to help the person learn and grow and to protect their reputation. I have found that addressing the obvious ends most rumor and gossip.

Example Number One: Pregnancy. Bill and Susan came to me one Sunday after church. They had been courting for almost a year. Observers had commented on how suitable they were. At first I assumed they were asking me about engagement and marriage. Nevertheless, the look on their face and their eyes told me otherwise.

Finding a place alone, he began to weep. Through his tears and groans he admitted that they had been immoral, and that she was now pregnant. We talked and prayed together for over an hour. I opened Scripture to them and explained that it was the immorality that was sin, that the pregnancy was under the sovereign purpose of God and this child was to be as cherished and valued as any. We talked about their marriage, keeping the child, and adoption possibilities.

Their last question was simple: What do we do once she is showing her pregnancy? Should we just move to another church? My answer was simple. Their family in Christ was the best place for them to be. Their sin would become evident to all. As soon as it did, people would talk. Talk would hurt the body. The only route to follow was a confession to their "group" within the church. This would clear the air, create support, and let them walk without fear. They agreed.

The morning of their confession came with agony. My teaching time was unfocused; their eyes were to the ground most of the time. At the end of our group gathering, I introduced the subject; they came forward, made their confession. We gathered a few leaders around them to pray. They called others to repent of their immorality. Many did. I never heard any more about it.

We chose to have their confession be to their peer group. We were a large church and they were nameless and faceless to the majority of members, but they were leaders in their peer group.

People rallied to them, supported them. Families helped them get ready for the child. They chose to marry and counsel was provided to prepare them – a very difficult task. In their early years of marriage, they needed much help.

I know some will hear this and think of the prurient interests of people in a voyeuristic culture. Isn't this playing into the hands of such indecent exposure and meddling hearts? It may be, but I still believe it is biblical. Read your New Testament carefully and you find there are times when names are named, where sin had become public and was dealt with publicly, including asking others to help with the problem.

I believe such addressing the obvious is the most helpful. On another occasion, a young woman stood before the whole church. She was well known and had also been immoral. She confessed, asked our forgiveness and help. Afterwards an older woman came to me, "I have seen these things swept under the rug for fifty years. All that did was create gossip. Now we can forgive and help." She did exactly that.

Example Number Two: The Scandal. Some sins are public knowledge because they are public record. You can read about them in the newspaper. Divorce is one such sin. Criminal activity is another. I have been part of dealing with too many divorces. I have also had a member involved in embezzlement.

Once again, when sin occurs publicly, the church is abuzz with talk. The couple they had known is never seen together: what happened? Their friend's name was in the paper: is it true or not?

I believe that faithfulness to the whole flock requires some public acknowledgment of the sin. This requires the wisdom of Solomon. Do we take sides in the divorce? Do we expose ourselves to the charge of libel? Do we convict a man in the church who is not yet proven guilty in the world? What is the role of the elders in such cases?

My goal is always to say enough to clear the air and to say only what can be verified. When one member was fired for embezzlement, he was willing to acknowledge his offense to the elders and to his peers. He admitted his wrong. We worked with him to establish a process of repayment to his corporation and to transition him into new work.

I have always viewed divorce as involving complex matters between the couple, but the party that initiates the divorce has crossed the line. I view them as the one to be dealt with. They are refusing to work any longer on the problem. We proceed with Matthew 18.

Now I must issue a word of caution: public exposure is only required when public knowledge is extensive. Not every divorce is scandalous. Some are very quiet. The people are not well known. We still follow Matthew 18.

Not all criminal charges are public. Some are lies. We stood with one couple who were charged with child abuse in their workplace. The investigation lasted two years. They insisted they were innocent. The charges were dismissed by the judge and the investigators admonished for sloppy work. The couple is grateful for our support through this time. It was never public, just a handful of elders. That is all that was needed.

There are factors of mercy as well. We do not need to bring the full weight of consequence on the person for their sin. Sometimes the error was great but the person needs to be given the opportunity to learn from their mistake, move on, and re-establish themselves. Public exposure would hurt their reputation and limit their opportunity to grow.

Example Number Three: Strife. There are times when a contention between members becomes widely known. Think of Euodia and Syntyche in Philippians. Usually this develops with two parties in major disagreement. They share their burden with their friends, who, in turn, tell others. Soon, the whole church is abuzz with the news. It is hard to tell who knows and who does not know. However, the division is infecting everyone.

What are we to do? The same thing Paul did with the ladies in Philippi. He speaks to the problems in front of the entire church.

I entreat Euodia and I entreat Syntyche to agree in the Lord. Yes, I ask you also, true companion, help these women, who have labored side by side with me in the gospel... (Phil. 4:2-3).

I saw a pastor do this once when I was a younger man. He did it at the Lord's Table. The conflict was between very prominent people in the church. It had to do with one of them not giving permission to their daughter to marry the son of the other couple. It spread widely.

The pastor, with their consent, invited them both down to the front seat. Then he addressed the whole congregation, giving the essence of the problem. Then he spoke to the couple. He charged them to work out their differences. He then called upon the congregation to stop talking about it but, rather, to encourage the couple by prayer to walk in a godly way. He encouraged them to apologize to each other for the hurt they had caused.

Then he prayed for them. What I remember most was that there was no more talk. There was nothing left to talk about.

Example Four: Rumors. Churches have people with loose tongues, whose business is to know everyone's business and to make sure others know the same, with a small amount of conjecture added. We cannot make it our business to track all rumors or even to allow the rumor-mongers to control when matters become public. Some rumors are best left to die. Paying attention to them gives credence to them and empowers their perpetrators.

A friend of mine was wickedly slandered by another elder. He was accused of striking the man. He spread the rumor to his friends. Many of them took up his cause. It spread to many in the church. I was new to the eldership so I watched how this was handled.

We asked these questions:

1. Is there any substance to the rumor?
2. Is the source of the rumor/slander clear?
3. Is acknowledging it going to give it greater power?

There was no substance to the rumor. The source was clear. The man responsible was admonished and asked to leave the church. He was a staff member and so firing was an option. He left the church. Nevertheless, the rumor was ignored publicly. It was felt that any attention paid to it would give it a dignity that it did not deserve. The accused's fellow elders stood with him and denied any possibility of the rumor being true, especially since they were supposed to have been in the room at the time. Within weeks it died, except in the hearts of a few who held it against the man, who had been falsely accused, for many years.

Spurgeon warned of rumor tracking, of always having an ear to the ground for the latest scuttlebutt. He said it will only lead to paranoia. People will talk. Let them talk. However, where there is fact, and that fact is public, and affects the whole church, it is best to address it publicly.

14

Tough Calls:
Dealing with Division

*There should be provision to speed up the
disciplinary process in cases of divisive persons.
If you linger too long over the process, you may
find your church divided*

Jay Adams

*****

Conflicts in the church are the corrosive agents
of a pastor's soul. No matter whether the issues
are large or small, strife breeds misery, sleepless
nights, and racing minds. They place us in the
awkward position of defending ourselves in
order to protect the church. They demand we
face angry people who feel entirely justified in
their anger.

Members walk out of services and meetings.
Elders resign from a Board in anger. Movements
against leadership are cultivated by gossips behind
the scenes. Theological exaggeration and agendas
tear churches apart. Members meddle in the

management of professional staff and hold informal investigations on decisions they do not like.

Dealing with individuals is central to church discipline. Guarding the church from schism is the larger concern with strife. It requires the courage only God can give.

My observation is that churches, even churches committed to disciplinary action, tolerate divisiveness more than any other sin. The longer they have known the one who troubles the church, the more likely they are to excuse it as something to be tolerated.

The New Testament knows no such toleration. The possibility of schism colors the entire Bible. Churches of the apostolic era faced the pain of factions within their ranks. Paul speaks of those who would, within a church, cause a faction to grow.

> I know that after I leave, savage wolves will come in among you and will not spare the flock. Even from your own number men will arise and distort the truth in order to draw away disciples after them. (Acts 20:29–30).

A stern warning is given against those who twist the truth. They do so to cause division.

> I urge you, brothers, to watch out for those who cause divisions and put obstacles in your way that are contrary to the teaching you have learned. Keep away from them. (Rom. 16:17).

Unity is cherished as a fruit of the Gospel.

> I appeal to you, brothers, in the name of our
> Lord Jesus Christ, that all of you agree with
> one another so that there may be no divisions
> among you and that you may be perfectly
> united in mind and thought. (1 Cor. 1:10).

Moreover, apostolic dread is expressed at the
prospect of a divided and contentious church:

> For I am afraid that when I come I may not
> find you as I want you to be, and you may
> not find me as you want me to be. I fear that
> there may be quarreling, jealousy, outbursts
> of anger, factions, slander, gossip, arrogance
> and disorder. (2 Cor. 12:20).

It is obvious that the Apostles take division
seriously. It is a sin against the very heart of our
salvation. The unity of the church in the truth that
is in Christ is the mark of her Savior's authenticity
(John 17:21, 23). Let's seek to understand it more
clearly.

Where does division come from? All division
has two roots: pride and talk. Pride compels us to
believe that our perception is the only accurate one.
We know better than anyone else, and others should
join us in our convictions. Talk spreads the fruit of
pride by quarrels, gossip, slander, suspicion, taking
sides, rebellion – always expressed in words.

> Pride only breeds quarrels, but wisdom is
> found in those who take advice. (Prov. 13:10).

> A perverse man stirs up dissension, and a gossip separates close friends. (Prov. 16:28).

> As charcoal to embers and as wood to fire, so is a quarrelsome man for kindling strife. (Prov. 26:21).

The talk of the divisive is always cowardly. They profess loyalty and then spread slander. They gather information and spread it to the shame of their enemies. They traffic in half truths and confidential information. They have no respect for privacy. They have no intention of loving protection but want "full disclosure" and no "secrets." Their most powerful argument is the argument from silence, a matter of confidentiality kept which they interpret as cover-up and deception. "Have you heard?" is their question. They most often are motivated by anger.

> Whenever one comes to see me, he speaks falsely, while his heart gathers slander; then he goes out and spreads it abroad. All my enemies whisper together against me. (Ps. 41:6–7).

> A gossip betrays a confidence, but a trustworthy man keeps a secret. (Prov. 11:13).

> A hot-tempered man stirs up dissension, but a patient man calms a quarrel. (Prov. 15:18).

> Hatred stirs up dissension, but love covers over all wrongs. (Prov. 10:12).

> An angry man stirs up dissension, and a hot-
> tempered one commits many sins.
> (Prov. 29:22).

The skill of the divisive is to use half truths to sow disharmony and suspicion. Their words sink deeply into the hearts of their followers and poison their attitudes to the enemy in question. Their behavior is one of the seven things God hates.

> The words of a gossip are like choice morsels;
> they go down to a man's inmost parts.
> (Prov. 26:22).

> There are six things the LORD hates, seven that are detestable to him: haughty eyes, a lying tongue, hands that shed innocent blood, a heart that devises wicked schemes, feet that are quick to rush into evil, a false witness who pours out lies and a man who stirs up dissension among brothers. (Prov. 6:16–19).

Finally, the divisive person loves tangents. They delight in feeding upon the side dishes of the faith and ignoring the healthy doctrine that engenders godliness. They love to explore the unsearchable and irresolvable questions of the faith and make them a subject of frequent conversation. Sadly, many a pastor is a dissenter at heart and relishes the tributaries of the faith rather than the vast river of Christ. We spend much of our ministry arguing for the fifth point of Calvinism or the depths of total depravity, the timing of the return of Christ in relation to the tribulation or the nature of pure church government. These always end in controversy.

> As I urged you when I went into Macedonia, stay there in Ephesus so that you may command certain men not to teach false doctrines any longer nor to devote themselves to myths and endless genealogies. These promote controversies rather than God's work – which is by faith. The goal of this command is love, which comes from a pure heart and a good conscience and a sincere faith. Some have wandered away from these and turned to meaningless talk. (1 Tim. 1:3–6)

> But avoid foolish controversies and genealogies and arguments and quarrels about the law, because these are unprofitable and useless. Warn a divisive person once, and then warn him a second time. After that, have nothing to do with him. You may be sure that such a man is warped and sinful; he is self-condemned. (Titus 3:9–11).

The question is this: What are we to do to cure division? I think the solution is the one most neglected. Be firm. Titus said it so well: warn them twice and stop them after that. Division and suspicion spread like a virus. Gossip always finds more and more ready ears to listen. The factious person may be a good friend, a long time member, a person angry at life; but they must be dealt with clearly and firmly. That is for the good of the body.

Scripture gives us the direction we have studied. Go to them, confirm the evidence, and take witnesses. Yet there seems to be an extra measure of seriousness in these cases. Why does Paul say, warn them twice and then have nothing to do with them? That is because the dissenter will take you down a road of endless discussion. They will confuse every issue and divert all your energies. Mark them. Take note of them. Do not follow them or give them too much attention. When they become factious, leading others against the unity of the church, cut them out of your life and the church if necessary.

What about the proper role of disagreement? Can't these principles be used to create a cult-like control of the members? Is there no place for differences being expressed in the body of Christ? Let us see what Scripture says.

First, the unity of the church is not a unity based upon agreement about every detail. The Apostles seemed comfortable that there would be some differences between believers and leaders (Rom. 14). What they insisted on was not uniformity at all points but absolute agreement in the "main thing" – the exaltation of Jesus Christ. Accepting those with whom we have differences is a mark of godliness. Not making much of peripherals like meat and drink is a measure of maturity.

Second, the doctrinal breadth of the letters of the Apostles is remarkably narrow. What I mean by that is those truths they seek to develop and expound are not many, but few. They have to do primarily with the person and work of Christ and its fruit in people's lives. There is no detailed exposition by Paul of the doctrine of the rapture of the church and its relationship to the anti-Christ. Peter does not give us a lengthy explanation of the word "elect" or "foreknowledge." There is little detail given as to what the gathered church did together – no order of service, no timetable. Here wisdom calls us to focus on the main things.

Next, the authority of leaders in the church is a delegated authority. It is wrapped up in Scripture and the respect of our people. Elders may not lord it over the flock and intimidate their consciences with the threat of dealing with all dissension. They are to submit to leaders as those who live and teach the Word. Wise shepherds lead people to conclusions and allow them time to grasp truth. We are not infallible.

Fourth, the problem is not whether to allow disagreement but how we disagree. Even matters of major concern in the theology of Scripture may be argued for with a gentle and peaceful spirit. The problem is not disagreement but flesh-driven disagreement. The flesh generates strife, suspicion, quarrelling, factions, divisions, envy. Where there is debate it must be with prayers that we might not sin against those with whom we disagree.

Fifth, here is the matter for discipline: disagreement in flesh-driven ways. Where the flesh takes over, the church must face the problem and remove the cancer from its midst. Do not try to win them over. Drive out the mocker and contention will cease.

I have learned this the hard way, more than once. Let me explain my mistakes. Jim was one of the most divisive people I have ever known in a church. He had a role in leadership. He conveyed at attitude of spiritual maturity. He seemed to walk with God. However, he was a busybody who had no sense of the boundaries of responsibility and authority.

He became involved with some of the elders and their personal lives. He loved to meddle and in doing so, he discovered that some of them had some struggles in marriage; others had bad attitudes toward fellow elders. He jumped into this with both feet. He called upon some of the leaders in the church to "deal with the sin in their midst." He stuck his nose in where it did not belong. He trafficked in opinions and attitudes and intruded into the staff. He created suspicion and derided any who did not agree with him as soft and compromising. He threatened public exposure of these "sins."

I made the mistake of trying to win him over, allowing him into my thinking and perspective, trying to give him a more patient perspective on people. All I did was feed his pride. Finally the leaders faced him squarely. In doing so we discovered how many tentacles he had created with the elders and how many divisions he had created by gossip and rumors. Almost the entire leadership team was tainted and mistrust set in that paralyzed our progress for months.

As a pastor I am trained to "rescue" people. I want to give them a third and fourth chance. My merciful side actually created room for his work of sowing discord and leading others to betray confidences.

As I said, this has happened more than once. Pastors can be taken in if they have a leaning toward excess kindness. Our kindness can create more problems than it will solve.

In the case of the divisive person they are to be identified and warned, twice at most, then isolated. Firm words about minding their own business and not interfering with the lives of others are the only language they will hear.

15

Exceptions and Abuses

The art of listening is crucial. Resist your yearning to win an argument. Listen with the intent of understanding. Let him know by your silences and by your sympathy to his needs that you come as friend rather than foe. Silences and grunts of understanding communicate love far better than pious protestations of it. And usually it is when the genuineness of your care dawns on him that his resistance will break down, and he will be relieved to get his sin off his chest. His conscience has been working all along. The Holy Spirit had seen to that. What he needed all the time was an understanding listener.

John White

* * * * *

One of my great fears in discussing church discipline is the misuse of these principles in the hands of churches which are wooden in their understanding of people and the Scriptures. The wisdom of church history stands as a huge warning against formulaic approaches to sin. The purpose of church discipline is not to run through a series of steps like an impersonal bureaucrat, but to minister Christ to the stumbling.

It takes wisdom. Wisdom is godly sense of knowing how to do things in a fallen world and among sinners. There are people who are very knowledgeable but have no wisdom. They cannot park a car. They run rough shod over others with the truth. We must be wise. Gregory of Nazianzus was the first to speak to the importance of wisdom in each case:

> As then the same medicine and the same food are not in every case administered to man's bodies, but a difference is made according to their degree of health or infirmity; so also are souls treated with varying instruction and guidance. ...Some are led by doctrine, others trained by example, some need the spur, others the curb; some are sluggish and hard to rouse to the good, and must be stirred by being smitten with the word; others are immodestly fervent in spirit, with impulses difficult to restrain like thoroughbred colts, who run wide of the turning post and to improve them the word must have a restraining and checking influence.[1]

---

1. Cited in *Skillful Shepherds* by Derek Tidball, Grand Rapids, Zondervan, 1986

Exceptions and Abuses

In this chapter I want to outline some principles of wisdom that may keep us from abuses in the exercise of discipline. It would be tragic if the instrument of Christ at making a community transformational became a tool of the devil in making it destructive.

Abuse No.1: Being a busybody

We have seen that our call to pursue holiness as local churches involves each other. We are brothers and sisters on this journey. We need each other. We are each called to judge ourselves. We are also called to help each other grow by pointing out sin.

However, this does not mean every sin. It does not mean focusing so much on others that we fail to see ourselves. I believe Jesus words about judging ourselves first are a great antidote to being hyper-critical of others (Matt. 7:1-5).

In the Thessalonian letters there seems to be an idleness among certain members. Their free time is turned to meddling in the affairs of others. Paul tells them to get to work. Fill their lives with right things and they will not have time to focus on others:

> For we hear that some among you walk in idleness, not busy at work, but busybodies. Now such persons we command and encourage in the Lord Jesus Christ to do their work quietly and to earn their own living. (2 Thess. 3:11–12).

Leave room for people to judge themselves. Leave room for the Holy Spirit to have his agenda in their lives. Be their encourager.

Abuse No.2: Redefining sin.

It is the endless tendency of humans to be their own gods and make up their own laws. I remember one occasion where our Board was discussing whether to allow a group of retired folks to rent our facility. When we heard that they enjoyed playing pinochle, one man objected, "That is sin!" When asked for a reference to prove his point, he demurred, "I don't know, but I know it is sin."

So shall we discipline for playing cards? What about driving a fancy car? Or wearing make-up? Or being overweight? No, the nature of discipline is for public and scandalous sins. Again, they must be sin as God defines it, not as our particular church does.

Jesus speaks severely against those who add to the Word of God and make their traditions equal to Scripture.

> And why do you break the commandment of God for the sake of your tradition?...for the sake of your tradition you have made void the word of God. You hypocrites! Well did Isaiah prophesy of you, when he said: 'This people honor me with their lips, but their heart is far from me; in vain do they worship me, teaching as doctrines the commandments of men.' (Matt. 15:3–9).

Let us be careful to deal with sin and not church-based taboos.

Abuse No.3: Not dealing with the Gospel.

I have preached for many years that the greatest enemy of the church is moralism. This is the belief that people would be better if they knew better and tried harder. It has the tone of the coach pushing his athletes to push more.

When we have a moralistic approach to dealing with sin in the church, we create a generation of hypocrites. People will run for cover because they can never measure up.

Moralistic church discipline is not seeking to reclaim or restore. It simply demands that people fall in line or be dismissed.

The Gospel is central to any environment of dealing with sin. It places us all on level ground. It tells us all that we are in need of Christ. It pushes us all to confess and forgive, as Christ has forgiven us. Under a Gospel-dominant influence, people become free to pursue their walk with Christ with honesty.

Abuse No.4: Misuse of authority.

We bring dirty hands to holy wars. History is replete with instances of the sad abuses of power in churches. Leaders can apply these principles with the idea that they will create a pure church. The outcome is a cult.

Wise and godly minds have reflected often on the limits of church authority. The best guards against abuse are these:

1. Make sure you have facts and verifiable evidence. Dismiss all hearsay. Listen only to eyewitness reports or confessions. Do not take anyone's word for it.

2. Do not act on anything for which there is not a simple passage of Scripture that explains the sin. Do not discipline people for breaking a church's taboo list.

3. Beware of thinking the practice of discipline will create a pure church. It will not.

4. Remember, authority in the church is vested in Scripture. The highest leaders are under the Word. Any authority they have is delegated and accountable to Christ and other believers. Leaders who will not be questioned are anti-Christian. Test all things by Scripture. Beware of leaders who speak often of their office and its powers. Godly leaders point you to Christ.

5. Note, there is proper use of authority, and guarding against abuse should not keep us from doing what is right out of fear.

Abuse No.5: Confusing the position of church staff with employment law.

The modern church is more of an institution than the informal family church of the early centuries. Churches have staff and associate pastors. How are we to view such men? Are they employees? If they are caught in misconduct what is to be done? There are some who see them as no different than employees in any company. They are to be corrected and if they do not comply, they are fired.

I believe the church must resist the organizational model at this point. The Senior Pastor may be called by the church. He may have the responsibility and authority to build his team of pastors in submission to and co-operation with his Board.

However, we should never construe this simply as the authority to "hire and fire." Staffs are godly people who are called to ministry. They serve the church of Christ, purchased with his blood. If a staff member or the senior pastor misbehaves, they are never to be summarily dismissed. They are to be treated according to the rules of Matthew 18. They may lose their job, but they are a member of Christ's body. Their spiritual well-being comes before the institutional life of the church.

One more thought should be offered here to elders who may be reading this. It has become more common in recent years for church boards to dismiss pastors or to pressure them out of their work. As you can see from this study, this is offensive to the whole process of truth-telling between brothers. It is both an abuse of authority and a loss of a sense of being the church. Pastors are not employees. They are first of all your brothers in Christ.

Sit down as soon as possible and work out a regular yearly gathering with your pastor to talk about his relationship with the church and effectiveness. Speak truthfully to each other. Put aside your fears and face him as a godly man. I know of men in ministry who would not respond to humble and clear communication that it is time for them to move into a new role. I also know of few who would be anything less than devastated by deceit and underhandedness. Honor Christ. Speak the truth with humility as a regular practice.

In each of these basic abuses, there are nuances. These are the ones I have seen most often. It is the role of pastors to oversee the flock and help them learn to function according to Scripture, with the Gospel, and without meddling. There will be mistakes along the way, but the Gospel addresses those as well.

Now let's talk about exceptions. Complexity gives us all headaches. God has given clarity. Man's sin muddies the waters. I have sought to give some pastoral per-spective on the practice of discipline. At first it appears to be cut and dried. In practice there are nuances and pitfalls aplenty. In this chapter I will seek to address some of the common questions related to church discipline which can be answered more briefly.

What do we do when someone withdraws during discipline?

Many churches practice a form of membership which is a voluntary association of a consenting person to the covenant of the church. The elders need to approach these situations wisely. Vindictiveness can easily become a motive.

Sometimes it is best to bring the process to a public conclusion. Sometimes it would do far greater damage. It is important to have a clearly defined membership covenant to which all members agree. That covenant must state clearly that their withdrawal from the church under discipline does not eliminate the possibility of public censure.

However, many churches have a public process of reporting changes in membership. Additions, deletions, transfers are a matter of public record. In this case I have used that vehicle to report to the church that the person withdrew under the process of discipline and it is recorded as such in the membership rolls.

This may seem to be "letting them get away with it" but I operate under the conviction that even church discipline is not the final word of God's judgment. God will right all wrongs and punish all unjudged sin. No one gets away with anything. At the same time some record must be made at whatever level of disclosure is consistent with the church's practice.

Sin is messy, terribly messy. Sometimes sin creates a scrambled egg, impossible to separate into yoke and white. As a pastor I have seen my share of impossible cases. Take the woman who accused her father of incest twenty-five years ago. Her evidence was a recovered memory. Her public accusation tore a family apart. Her Christian counselor insisted this was a time for discipline. Her father denied the accusation. There was no corroborating evidence. He wanted to be publicly vindicated. What to do?

I remember the day a young lady, a mother of three, came to me with a heavy heart. She was dreadfully afraid. Her husband was gone at night, often late. She discovered a bandana and a knife in the glove compartment of his car. I was counseling him for sexual addiction, an arrangement in which he had asked me not to tell her his problem. What to do?

I have rarely if ever found a situation that was not complicated. However, I have also been faced with problems that no set of principles seemed to clarify. There are always mitigating circumstances.

I have turned in those times to a passage in the Old Testament:

> If cases come before your courts that are too difficult for you to judge – whether bloodshed, lawsuits or assaults – take them to the place the LORD your God will choose. Go to the priests, who are Levites, and to the judge who is in office at that time. Inquire of them and they will give you the verdict. You must act according to the decisions they give you at the place the LORD will choose. Be careful to do everything they direct you to do. Act according to the law they teach you and the decisions they give you. Do not turn aside from what they tell you, to the right or to the left. (Deut. 17:8-11).

The first time I read those words, I just about shouted for relief. Here was an acknowledgment by God that there are inscrutable messes with insufficient clarity and mitigating circumstances and yet something must be done.

The simple direction here is this: involve the most godly people and make a decision. That decision shall stand and is to be respected. The worst thing may be to do nothing. The problem will not go away. Deal with it. Determine a verdict, guilty or innocent, and trust God.

All this is a long introduction to my belief that sometimes, rarely, circumstances prohibit the completion of a disciplinary process. This primarily takes place when a greater evil will result from the public censure of the person. And by greater evil I do not mean slander or hostility for our obedience, but life-threatening responses.

Let's take the threat of suicide. More than once the hand of God upon the rebellious heart has brought them to a point of despair in the midst of the disciplinary process. David says, "Day and night your hand was heavy upon me". (Ps. 32:3–4). When God wants to make us miserable to bring us to repentance, he knows exactly what nerve to strike.

More than once the increasing pressures of the process of challenging the sin according to Scripture has pushed a "patient" over the edge. They have fallen into deep depression and despair, and attempted suicide. In those cases I believe the path of wisdom is to stop the level of exposure and for the elders to act quietly to remove that person from the church in the name of Christ.

There may also be a threat of violence. Abusive husbands, under the pressure of church admonition, can inflict considerable damage to a wife or a child. Great care needs to be given here lest we provoke a violent person to harm others in the name of "church discipline." This requires at least some form of legal action to protect the spouse or children.

This can be a difficult decision as it exposes the church to the possibility of rumor. It may look to some like the leaders are inconsistent. And explanations cannot be given. I have found that making myself available to the people who are concerned for a one-to-one conference is often very helpful. Without divulging confidences they can be assured of the desire for a process with integrity.

When I was in training for ministry I was told that working principles from Scripture into life was a matter of dealing with the shades of grey. The clarity of Scripture must be applied with wisdom and there are times when principles seem to conflict with each other in application. The promise of James is an anchor at such times. God gives wisdom, decisions must be made, and action taken or not taken.

16

A Plea for Order

Preaching is a wonderful privilege for the pastor or elder of a church. Much attention is given to making us good preachers. Important as preaching is, it is not enough. I close with an appeal for elders and pastors to recover the components of ministry vital to a disciplined local congregation.

I am a father of three. I teach my children by general instruction and by very specific application of principle to life. It is not enough to teach. There must be the enforcement of the truth in discipline, rebuke, admonition.

When my people come to hear me preach, they often dodge the arrows of the Word. They find that what I have said has great application to someone else. They find inspiration in my words. But rarely do they see how it speaks to them.

One Sunday I spoke on gossip. After the service a man came to me and told me a terribly demeaning story about another man in the church. I told him this was the gossip I had been speaking of. He paused and noted he had never thought of it that way!

When my people gather with their friends on Sunday they talk in generalities. They rarely get down to the details of life and how Scripture applies to them. When they hear a word of bitterness or an inappropriate piece of humor, they do not correct or graciously call the person to holiness. They dodge the personal and the specific.

Paul said that he trained people like a father trains his children, admonishing and teaching them, exhorting and encouraging them (Col. 1:28–9). He did this eyeball to eyeball, face to face. Unless we do the same in the church and call our people to relationships of spiritual challenge, the churches we serve will always be flabby and disordered.

I tell my fellow pastors that the real progress in ministry takes place in the trench war with sin as we rub shoulders with each other. Hebrews 3:12-13 gives us no other choice. My life and words and friendships are to be sharpening the lives of all involved to be more earnest followers of Christ. We cannot be bashful or timid. The holiness of the church depends on it. The Gospel's advance depends on it. Preaching must be followed by hands on discipleship and toil in the lives of our flock.

But is this what churches do? Is it what pastors do? I do not find it so. Most pastors I know of function without anyone involved in their lives helping them walk in godliness. They have no pastor of their own souls.

I want to plead first of all for pastors to live in these truths themselves. How many men will falter and quit ministry in discouragement before we understand that we cannot do it alone? How many will fall into immorality before we expect our spiritual leaders to watch over their own spirituality?

Pastors, find one or two men, fellow pastors if need be, and meet with them to talk about your soul. Forget the fun stuff of talking theology and avoiding your own heart. Lay out your agenda. Deal with your souls in the way you expect your congregation to allow you to deal with them. Take the Wesleyan cell group questions and discuss them. They start with easy ones: how have you sinned this past week? In what are you being tempted? Then they get personal. Encourage each other in the Gospel.

Then, establish clear constitutional guidelines for the exercise of these truths in your life as a church. Legal problems may arise in the process of discipline. My legal counsel has always said the same thing: there needs to be a simple outline of the process and its practice in the life of the church stated in the bylaws or constitution of the church. Every member needs to give their consent to this. It must be practiced consistently.

Teach your lay leaders these principles. More than that, encourage them toward highly transparent and accountable friendships. If the leaders do not act like they think this is important, what do you think the people will do?

Teach your people and give them tools by which to practice. Teach them again. Model it. Remind them again. This is scary for most. It will take years to learn this pattern. It is worth it. It will save the church from a good measure of unreality and phoniness. It will save the church from some scandal.

You may say, the church is not ready for this. I tend to agree with Richard Baxter: how can we not be ready for obedience? This is the command of God, practiced among the earliest churches of the Apostolic era. But you must teach it, get ownership, and pray for courage to obey.

Your church may resist mightily. You will need to be wise as a serpent and harmless as a dove. I have learned that there are churches which, by habitual walking in lies and deceit, by consistently failing to deal with sin forthrightly, are filled with deadness and cancer. This process of forming a transformational community is all about walking in the light. People who are used to the darkness will flee from the light.

Lead them wisely and well. The best way to bring change to such a place is by prayer. Bring them to pray. Let them be still before God and wait upon him. Preach the Gospel to them so they drop their fears and open up to the Spirit. Practice a quiet and calm truthfulness and directness of communication. Gently call them to deal with each other directly. Disciple them one at a time in the Gospel. If one and then another begin to walk in the light personally, it may spread.

Remember, we are seeking to be an expression of the great body of Christ. Our local assemblies can be reminded often of all that Jesus has done for them and all that they are. We all battle sin, but Christ has given us the simple means, through godly relationships, to help each other along the way.

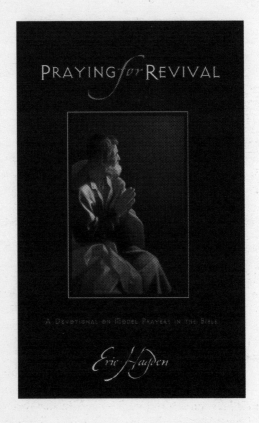

PRAYING for REVIVAL

A DEVOTIONAL ON MODEL PRAYERS IN THE BIBLE

Eric Hayden

Praying for Revival

A Devotional on Model Prayers in the Bible
Eric Hayden

As Christians, we all long for Revival. We read accounts of revivals in the past with a mildly repressed envy. We wish we would experience them in our local situation but having seen new methods come and go, too often we resign ourselves to failure.

Eric Hayden reminds us of the necessity of prayer when we desire revival. Looking at the thirty-five prayers for revival found in the bible Hayden gives us a series of short studies on Revival and Prayer. With a chapter for each prayer we are shown how Prayer and Revival are intricately linked in Scripture and consequently in our every day lives. This is a wonderful book that will help revive in us the Biblical attitude to revival, and remind us that Revival comes from God himself.

"Eric Hayden understands true revival. He also understands that true revival usually comes when God's people pray for the gift of the Spirit biblically and passionately. This book should be commended to church leaders the world over. It is both clear headed and warm hearted."

John H. Armstrong, President,
Reformation & Revival Ministries

Eric Hayden is a retired Baptist Minister with one of his previous charges having been Spurgeon's Metropolitan Tabernacle, London.

ISBN 1 85792 686 2

T. M. MOORE

Think of T.M. Moore's work as high-octane fuel . . I pray it will ignite churches with longing for a true visitation of God in our time.

John Armstrong

PREPARING YOUR CHURCH FOR

REVIVAL

Preparing your Church for Revival

T.M. Moore

We all long for revival, but we tend to pray for it to come without being completely sure what precisely revival is. This book will be a revitalising aid to those of us who desire revived spiritual life for our churches. T.M. Moore offer practical advice on steps, each with secure scriptural foundations, that we can take to prepare our churches for the sovereign work that is revival. This book is clear that there is no conflict between revival being a work of God and the continued and urgent need for God's people to earnestly pray for its appearance.

With practical guides to prayer for revival T.M. Moore realises the need for balance and succeeds in providing a book that will help us to refocus on revival, and will prepare our souls and our churches for the mighty work of a Sovereign and loving God.

'Think of T. M. Moore's work as high-octane fuel, written by a man who loves the church of Jesus Christ and longs to see her full of his glory once again. I pray his 'fuel' will ignite churches with longing for a true visitation of God in our time.'

**John H. Armstrong, President,
Reformation & Revival Ministries**

T. M. Moore is Pastor of Teaching Ministries at Cedar Springs Presbyterian Church in Knoxville, TN.

ISBN 1 85792 698 6

Revive Us Again
Biblical Insights for Encouraging Spiritual Renewal

Walter C Kaiser Jr

Revive Us Again
Biblical Principles for Revival Today
Walter C Kaiser Jr.

It only takes a look at the evening news for us to realise that there is much wrong with this world of ours. The sins of Greed, Lust, Violence and Corruption are rife in all sections of our society. Christians are becoming at best an irrelevance and at worst a persecuted minority.

Walter C Kaiser Jr. suggests the one answer to these pressing problems, revival. Not a foot-stomping, soul-saving series of meetings, but an individual believer's refocusing on God as the centre of life.

With his usual scholarship and vision Dr Walter C. Kaiser Jr. reveals spiritual principles inherent in the great awakenings of the Bible and shows us how to prepare the way for revival today. Revivals like those led by Moses and by John the Baptist provide us with clear examples of what God can do when His sovereign will is acknowledged and obeyed. Read this book and help prepare the way for revival in your community, your church and most importantly your heart.

Dr Walter C Kaiser Jr. is Colman M.Mockler Distinguished Professor of Old Testament and President of Gordon-Conwell Theological Seminary.

ISBN 1 85792 687 0

The Little Book Of...
Things You Should Know About
MINISTRY

Reid Ferguson

Foreword by John Armstrong

The Little Book of things you should know about Ministry
Reid Ferguson

With short and thought-provoking chapters this book will enable you to think through the issues involved in leading a congregation and enable you to serve your flock with greater success.

'... refreshingly candid, consistently thought provoking, and eminently practical.'

Phillip R. Johnson
Executive Director, Grace to You Ministries

'When we are dispirited; when we feel unappreciated, opposed or unsupported; the wisest responses can be considered from these pages. Read a chapter every week!'

C. Peter White,
Sandyford Henderson Memorial Church,
Glasgow, Scotland

'...the compassion of the pastor's heart is evident in every thought'

Ken Jones,
Alliance of Confessing Evangelicals

Reid Ferguson is a native of Rochester NY. A third generation minister, he has been at the independent, Evangelical Church of Fairport, Rochester for 27 years.

ISBN 1 85792 786 9

"Surely the finest book to date on this difficult subject"
John MacArthur Jnr

THE STAIN THAT STAYS

The Church's response to the sexual misconduct of its leaders

John H. Armstrong
Foreword by R. Kent Hughes

The Stain that Stays

The Church's response to the sexual misconduct of its leaders.

John H. Armstrong

What should happen to pastors who fall to sexual misconduct? Should they return, repentant, to their pulpits within weeks or months – or should they return at all?

"This is a pastoral letter from a sinner to sinners, composed with gracious humility. Above all The Stain that Stays is biblical. John Armstrong has done his homework. It deserves a wide reading by pastors, denomination leaders, church elders, and all who love the church."

R. Kent Hughes

"This book is a needed corrective to the growing trend to restore fallen ministers into pastoral leadership. Whether one agrees with all John Armstrong's conclusions, he makes a case that desperately needs to be heard."

Erwin Lutzer

"Armstrong has left no stone unturned and yet he has thrown no stones at fallen brothers. The book reflects a properly pastoral tone and a broken heart."

Al Mohler

"Surely the finest book to date on this difficult subject"
John MacArthur Jnr

ISBN 1 85792 5831

Reformation & Revival Ministries

Reformation & Revival Ministries, in partnership with Christian Focus Publications, has an imprint line of books for the purpose of providing resources for the reformation of the Christian church through the life and work of Christian leaders. Our goal is to publish and distribute new works of pastoral and theological substance aimed at reforming the leadership, life and vision of the church around the world.

Reformation & Revival Ministries was incorporated in 1991, through the labors of John H. Armstrong, a pastor for the previous twenty-one years, to serve the church as an educational and evangelistic resource. The desire from the beginning has been to encourage doctrinal and ethical reformation joined with informed prayer for spiritual awakening. The foundational convictions of the ministry can be summarized in the great truths of the sixteenth century Protestant Reformation and evangelical revivals of the 18th & 19th centuries.

To accomplish this vision the ministry publishes a quarterly journal, *Reformation & Revival Journal*, designed for pastors and serious readers of theology and church renewal. A more popular magazine, *Viewpoint*, is published six times a year. The ministry also has an extensive array of books and tapes.

Dr. Armstrong speaks in conferences, local churches and various ministerial groups across the

United States and abroad. The ministry has a no debt policy and is financed only by the gifts of interested people. The policy is to make needs known only to those who ask, believing that God provides as he will, where he will, and when he will. An office and support staff operate the ministry in suburban Chicago.

Further information on the ministry and resources can be found at -

Reformation & Revival Ministries
P. O. Box 88216
Carol Stream, Illinois 60188
Tel: (630) 980-1810
Fax: (630) 980-1820

E-mail: RRMinistry@aol.com
Web: www.reformationrevival.com

Christian Focus Publications
We publish books for all ages.

STAYING FAITHFUL
In dependence upon God we seek to help make his
infallible word, the Bible, relevant. Our aim is to ensure
that the Lord Jesus Christ is presented as the only hope to
obtain forgiveness of sin, live a useful life, and look
forward to heaven with him.

REACHING OUT
Christ's last command requires us to reach out to our world
with his gospel. We seek to help fulfil that by publishing
books that point people towards Jesus and for them to
develop a Christ-like maturity. We aim to equip all levels
of readers for life, work, ministry and mission.

Books in our adult range are published in three imprints:-
Christian Focus contains popular works including
biographies, commentaries, basic doctrine, and
Christian living. Our children's books are also
published in this imprint.
Christian Heritage contains classic writings from the
past.
Mentor focuses on books written at a level suitable
for Bible College and seminary students, pastors, and
other serious readers; the imprint includes
commentaries, doctrinal studies, examination of
current issues, and church history.

Christian Focus Publications, Ltd
Geanies House, Fearn, Ross-shire,
IV20 1TW, Scotland, United Kingdom
info@christianfocus.com

www.christianfocus.com